Flower Arranging
Without Flowers

Flower Arranging Without Flowers

and hundreds of other garden club secrets that nobody ever tells you

Illustrated by Jeanne, Sean and Cyn O'Neill

by Jeanne Lamb O'Neill

The Bobbs-Merrill Company, Inc.

Indianapolis / New York

Designed by Ingrid Beckman
Manufactured in the United States of America

First printing

Library of Congress Cataloging in Publication Data

O'Neill, Jeanne Lamb.

  Flower arranging without flowers.
  1. Flower arrangement. 2. Design, Decorative—
Plant forms. I. Title.
SB449.058 1976   745.92   74–17675
ISBN 0–672–52008–7

For my mother,
who always knew I could
type in gardening gloves

Contents

Acknowledgments

IT WOULD BE IMPOSSIBLE to pinpoint precisely who I stole what from where. With my heart on my sleeve, as well as in my mouth, I offer a blanket thank you to all the expert writers, teachers, and lecturers who have shared their know-how with me. A listing of some of my favorite authors is provided at the back of this book.

Specifically, I thank Stanley Schuler, whose *How to Grow Almost Everything* is the only gardening book I own; Irma H. Crawmer, who taught me more in three lessons than Madame La Zonga; Bernice Fitz-Gibbon, who taught me how to write WORDS without flowers; and my dear friend Les Forester, who kept my typewriter from getting rusty.

My warmest thanks to the two most talented arrangers I know—Audrey Patterson (pages 30, 59, and 110), who could paper her entire home with blue ribbons and state and national awards and who kindly checked these pages for bloopers; and Joyce Hayes (pages 6, 9, and 15), who wouldn't be caught dead in a garden club. Also Betty Kelly, the perfect editor; Emilie

Jacobson, the perfect agent; Jean Dietrich, the perfect typist, and (and that's a big "and") my perfect family.

For assorted reasons, I thank Nancy Becker, Dorrie Byrne, Marcia FitzGibbon, Harriet Flotte, Mark Forester, Ruth Gleese, Verna King, the Bob Knights, Gail Le Beau, Grace M. O'Neill, the Willard Smiths, Hoddy Stickle, Emily Ulrich, and Syl Vaughn. Thanks, too, to all of my ex-associates in Halten Garden Club, especially Willette Bland, Frances Huber, and Pauline Leiter.

Most especially, I thank Serena S. Bridges, who is undoubtedly now telling the head gardener of the Elysian fields how to grow daffodils.

Introduction

===========

ALL MY LIFE I'VE WANTED not to write a book. I wrote this one because no one else ever did, in all the years I needed it.

Where was *Flower Arranging Without Flowers* when I was young and foolish? Why didn't somebody tell me I could have flowers when I couldn't afford flowers? Why didn't somebody tell me how to do an "all-green" or bake a daffodil or dazzle my dinner guests with just three cheap glads? All I needed were a few friendly, girl-to-girl tips. All I got were snooty ten-pound full-color volumes that scared the *helleborus* out of me. All those dreary diagrams. All those cranky rules and tight-lipped regulations. All those *flowers*. No wonder I didn't get beyond jonquils in a jelly glass for twenty-five years.

Well, I'm still not above jonquils in a jelly glass. But, one way or another, I've learned a few thousand tricks besides. I've spent years picking the brains of the experts. I've kept my eyes and ears open at flower shows, flower-arranging lectures, demonstrations, and workshops. I've been obnoxiously nosy on house-and-garden tours, not to mention at private dinner parties. I even belonged to a garden club once. Happily, for all my expert-type expertise, I'm still not what anyone could call an Expert. I'm just an over-grown amateur, and if I want to spill the garden-club beans, what ho? (Experts don't mean to be stingy with their secrets—they've just forgotten what it's like to be poor and dumb.)

Okay. The big, beautiful, deep dark secret of arranging that everybody but you knows is this—you don't need flowers. How's that again? How on earth can you flower-arrange without *flowers?* That's what the next fourteen chapters are all about. But, in a cockleshell, here's what I mean by flower arranging without flowers.

First of all, I mean just what I say—without a single blooming bloom. If you've been to any flower shows lately, you know that just plain flowers are as old as your Easter hat. "In" arrangers use almost anything *but*—fruits and vegetables, green leaves, bare branches, potted plants, driftwood, fungi, roots, grasses, stones, pinecones, seeds and weeds—not to mention plumber's pipes, furnace filters, and "finds" from the city dump. If garden clubbers don't need flowers, why should you?

I also mean flower arranging without *fresh* flowers. Isn't that what most people mean by flowers? Even if you can't afford florist's roses and don't have a garden, you can fill the house with flowers all year round by drying your own or making your own frankly-fakes.

More than that, I mean flower arranging without spending money on flowers. Isn't that most people's hang-up? I mean flower arranging with scot-free wildflowers from the field. I mean flower arranging without any flowers to speak of, Japanese style. Even if you don't know Ikebana from your elbow (and don't care if you never do), you can do beautiful "your own thing" arrangements with just one flower or two. To me, anything less than half a dozen flowers is the same as none. I mean flower arranging without spending more than a dollar, or two at the most. To me, that's not too much for a smart girl to hide in her grocery bill.

Most of all, I mean fool-the-eye flower arranging—with half as many flowers and twice the effect. Learn how to put your flowers where they'll count the most, and even if you don't have a green thumb, a greenhouse, or a green, growing bank account, people will *think* you do.

Of course, part of the game of flower arranging "without flow-ers" is knowing where to buy flowers cheaper, how to make flowers last longer, what to put them in, how to make them stay put, and what's "in" in flower arranging today. That's why you'll find hundreds of inside garden-club tips in Section Three and scattered throughout the book.

You might call this "the poor girl's flower-arranging book." It was written for poor girls because there are more poor girls than rich girls in the world, especially by my definition. In my book, a poor girl is any girl who can't afford flowers 365 days a year. But there are all kinds of poor girls. This book is for young girls and old girls, city girls and country girls, career girls and house-wives. It's even for *rich* little poor girls (you know who you are, you with the plastic geraniums in your Grecian urns). Especially, it's for brides. More especially, it's for lazy girls, like myself.

Mind you, this isn't a how-to-arrange book. It's a what-to-ar-range book. First things first. What good are the rules for a lush Victorian mass arrangement if you don't have six dozen roses to put in it? Besides, that's what all the *other* books are about. By all means, study the splendid flower-arranging tomes in your library, the first year you get a chance. By the time you're ninety, you too will know all about color, balance, dominance, contrast, rhythm, proportion, and scale. In the meantime, stop worrying and start arranging. Arrange something, anything, and, as you'll see, "nothing." (If I'd worried about rules, most of the arrangements in this book would have died on the drawing board.)

Remember, this isn't a do-or-die flower-show competition; it's your very own home. The saddest woman I know is the ardent flower lover who joined a garden club to become a better arranger —and hasn't had a flower in the house since. *They* might catch her with a lopsided Hogarth S-curve.

Part One

How to Flower-Arrange Without Flowers

1

Green Is Beautiful

I USED TO THINK "greens" were something you used only at Christmas. I thought florists put "greens" in their boxes just to make the flowers look like more. And then I discovered the best friend a poor flower arranger ever had—the "all-green arrangement." If you never learn another look-Ma!-no-flowers trick, learn to do an "all-green" and you'll be set for life.

The almighty "all-green"

Have you ever heard of an "all-green"? Don't worry, nobody else has either. It's an "inside" arrangement, one of those sneaky secrets that garden clubbers like to hug to their bosoms. What it is is just what it sounds like—an arrangement of leaves, all leaves and nothing but leaves—and don't snoot it till you try it. Garden clubbers win "blues" with "all-greens." People go to flower-

3

arranging school to study "all-greens." All-foliage arrangements are not only perfectly respectable; they're also perfectly beautiful, and indecently simple. Anyone can make one, any time of the year.

What's good about greens?

If you think about it, greens have everything going for them. In the first place, they're cheap. If you can't gather them right in your own backyard or by the wayside, you can't go broke at the florist's, either. Secondly, like all good friends, greens are there when you need them. They're always in season, twelve months of the year. No matter what part of the country you live in, there's always *something* green to be picked. What's more, greens are practically eternal. An all-green arrangement can last for weeks or even months, depending on what you pick and how faithful you are at water-changing. Best of all, leaves are fun to arrange. It's normal to quiver and quake over fancy-priced hothouse flowers, but how can you get uptight about a bunch of greens?

Even better than flowers, yet?

I won't pretend that an armful of leaves is more thrilling than a truckload of tulips. Obviously, the best reason for using greens is that greens are all you've got. Greens are to see you through the long, hard winter when your garden is dead and buried. Greens are to save your life when the price of pink carnations is out of sight. But don't think an all-green arrangement is purely and simply a desperation measure. It could be a stroke of genius.

For instance, on a hot, sweltering August day, what could be cooler, frostier, more soul-soothing than an "all-green"? Or, if you itch to brighten up your husband's den or office but he can't stand sissy bouquets, what better answer than an "all-green"? For instance, if you've just redone the living room in green, gold, and white, what could be more chic than an arrangement to match? Or if you've gone in for really wild colors, an "all-green" may be the only nonclashing solution.

Here's another thought: When you're trying to cheer up friends in the hospital or elderly shut-ins, bunches of hot, bright flowers are likely to make them feel even worse. Chances are, friends or family are just too polite to say so. Wouldn't a bowl of restful greens be more thoughtful?

But what can you do with a bunch of greens?

You can do almost anything with leaves that you can do with flowers. If you want to be technical, you can do a vertical, horizontal, line-mass, Hogarth curve, crescent, symmetrical, asymmetrical, Ikebana, tussy-mussy, or any other standard arrangement in the book. In plain language, you can do a gay "little nothing" for the breakfast table (use sprigs of glistening boxwood instead of marigolds or pansies). You can create a tall, show-off arrangement for the foyer (use branches of cocculus with pittosporum instead of banal gladioli). Or you can spend hours fussing over a fancy dinner-party arrangement (there are just as many mixed greens around as there are mixed flowers).

All-green doesn't mean all-dull

Have you ever noticed how many different shades of green there are in the world? Any artist can tell you there's no such thing as green-green. So can any decorator. Fabled Billy Baldwin, who obviously loves flowers, writes lyrically of "a variety of greens that run from pale silver-dust green to flute notes of piercing emerald."* Just look out the window and count the greens. There are sunny yellow-greens and frosty blue-greens, ethereal silver-greens and glossy green-blacks, pinkish greens, brownish greens, coppery greens, purply greens, and dozens of

*Billy Baldwin Remembers, Harcourt Brace Jovanovich, New York and London, 1974 (and a great book to own).

shades in between. There are tender young pale greens; rich, full-bodied bright greens; and deep, brooding dark greens. And those are just the solid-color greens—don't forget multicolor greens and greens with speckles, stripes, and polka dots.

Leaves come in different shapes, too, just like flowers—fat, skinny, round, oval, swordlike, feathery, curly, pointy. They also have different "personalities," just like flowers. You don't have to carry on out loud about it, but with a little imagination you'll find leaves that are dainty or dramatic, shy or bold, elegant or folksy. And when it comes to variety in texture, leaves have it all over flowers—they may be sleek, coarse, velvety, furry, rubbery, satiny, prickly, leathery, feathery, you name it. There's a whole world of texture in needled evergreens alone. Never think a leaf is a leaf is a leaf—even Chinese evergreens don't all look alike.

Come to think of it, green is a color, just like pink and orange. In fact, some of the prettiest *flowers* that grow are green. Everybody knows green bells of Ireland, but did you know that there are green zinnias, green coralbells, green tulips, green flowering tobacco, and even green gladioli? Of course it's strictly taboo to use flowers in an "all-green" at a flower show, but who cares if you cheat at home? A bevy of beautiful greens spiked with bright

chartreuse Envy zinnias makes a spectacular special-occasion arrangement. (The yellow-speckled variegated aucuba, swordlike yucca and green zinnias are homegrown, but you could substitute other garden greens for the aucuba and use iris leaves or sansevieria from a houseplant instead of yucca. In fact, you could make do with just five Envy zinnias, or substitute a pale, contrasting-textured green such as holly, hemlock or sedum. On the other hand, you could fill out the illustrated bouquet to sinful lavishness with clouds of snowy baby's breath—or a look-alike wildflower whose name I don't know that thrives in midsummer at the same time as zinnias. P.S.: Green zinnias dry nicely, and can perk up your foliage arrangements all winter long. There's no law against mixing dried materials with fresh, you know.)

Where to start and when to stop

The first step in making an all-green arrangement is to open your eyes. Stop taking greenery for granted. Go out and take a good garden-clubby look at the bushes, trees, and plants around you. Almost anything green except grass is fair game for your clippers. Once you start thinking green, you won't know where to start snipping first.

But please don't snip away like a drunken barber. Think before you cut, so that you don't spoil the shape of a precious shrub. (The Japanese will circle a tree for hours, literally, before selecting a single branch.) Use good, sharp clippers. And cut less than you think you'll need. It's much easier to go back for more than to Scotch-tape your rejects back on.

Generally speaking, "less is more" in an all-green arrangement. Or, to use an old flower-arranging motto: "When in doubt, leave it out." Don't overstuff your container just because you've got greens to burn. Give your leaves room to breathe, and leave some open spaces for light to shine through. And remember—nature can nearly always be improved upon. If you don't like the look of this leaf or that—prune, prune away. After all, they're "only" greens.

Greens for "have-not" homeowners

I said this is a what-to-arrange book, so let's get down to business. If you're a dewy-eyed bride in your first new house, you don't have century-old elms and boxwood as big as a boxcar. You're probably lucky to have grass. But no matter how young and callow your landscaping may be, I'll bet you have greens. You have a tree, don't you? And at least a few bushes, courtesy of the builder, to hide the foundation? Believe it or not, those ordinary, everyday outdoor bushes are just as arrangeable as roses and daffodils.

Take *yew*, for instance. That's the most common, ordinary, everyday bush I know. For years I walked past our foundation yews with my nose in the air. I had to join a garden club to learn that plain old yew (they call it *taxus*) is fit to sit on my dining room table. And have you ever thought of bringing *hemlock* into the house? I've seen flower arrangers with a garden full of flowers choose hemlock boughs instead. Have you ever thought of "arranging" branches of lowly *privet?* Never mind if other people throw away their hedge clippings—the experts put privet (they call it *ligustrum*) in their best silver bowls.

If privet and yew and hemlock are okay with the powers that be, what on earth *isn't?* Grab your clippers and explore your own backyard. You may find bushes you didn't know you had. You may even find a bush that isn't a yew. Don't worry if you don't know what it's called; if it's green, growing, and yours, use it. And don't worry about arranging by the book. You're not trying to do justice to a fortune in exotic materials—you're struggling with the bottom of the barrel, poor dear. Just pick your greens, pick a container that seems appropriate to you—and arrange. If you like it and your husband doesn't throw it at you, that's enough for openers.

To get you started, here are a few simpleminded suggestions for bottom-of-the-barrel greens:

• Toss an armful of graceful, tender-tipped hemlock boughs into a tall, simple cylinder (it's called a *spill*).

• Tuck snippets of glossy green privet, cut into different lengths, into an antique tea caddy or cigarette box; add a few pale yellow tree buds.

• Combine tall spikes of dark green yew with chubby clumps of clipped pine and geranium leaves in a china cup, or add privet and feathery cedar to boughs of yew in a low bowl.

Greens for "haves" who don't know what they've got

See? All you need is a yew or two to do an "all-green." But, happily, newlyweds turn into over-thirty's, acorns into oaks, and builders' muddy lots into lush green plantings. Let's assume you're an old, settled homeowner with the average number of old, settled trees and bushes in your yard. Do you ever look at them twice? Some of the smartest arrangers I know can't see their trees for their flowers. All summer long they'll fill the house with enormous, eye-popping bouquets, but, come the first frost, their containers go into mothballs. They have a fortune in greenery outside but don't even know it. I'll bet my bottom dahlia you do, too.

When I say a fortune in greenery, I don't mean rare, exotic specimen plantings. I'm talking about the same ordinary bushes that you and I and your Aunt Harriet have. I'm sure you have at least one, if not all, of the good old standbys—*rhododendron, laurel, azalea.* Remember when you used to *buy* rhododendron leaves for your first apartment? Just because they're free doesn't make them any less glossy, gleaming, and glamorous. The same goes for laurel leaves. And do you forget all about your azaleas except when they're bursting with bloom? Garden clubbers love azalea foliage and use it in their snootiest flower-show entries.

How about *boxwood?* Sure, boxwood is handy for filling in "holes" in flower arrangements, but it's even dandier in all-green arrangements. So is the "poor girl's boxwood," *Japanese holly*— and almost any other broad-leaved evergreen you may have.

But the most neglected stepchildren in your yard are probably the needled evergreens—the so-called Christmas tree greens like *pine, cedar, spruce,* and *hemlock.* Why does everybody have a mental block about evergreens? Who says you can only cut Christmas greens in December? They're just as beautiful the other eleven months. By all means, deck the halls with boughs

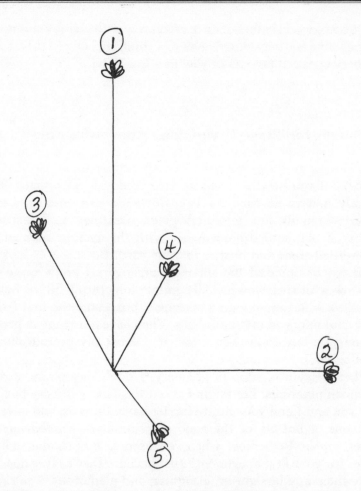

of *holly* in the merry month of May—the first young baby-green shoots are luscious in springtime arrangements.

While you're out beating the bushes for greens, don't overlook the *ivy* on the walls—not to mention the *pachysandra* on the ground. Pachysandra has a lovely leaf if you look at it and is especially good for stuffing into fruit arrangements. Check your flowerbeds for treasures you may never have thought of using. Curly, swirly *hosta* (or *funkia*) leaves, especially the variegated kind, are worth their weight in gold. *Sedum* flowers aren't much to look at, but the fleshy, pale green leaf stalks are fascinating. Steal a few leaves from a *geranium* that isn't blooming the way it should. Do you happen to grow *curly mint*? It's great in arrangements as well as on the dinner plate; you can also dry or freeze it.

And don't forget that *iris, lily of the valley,* and *peony* leaves stay fresh and green long after the flowers have died.

Have you seen the new trick of arranging flowers in a potpourri of little jars and bottles instead of in the usual old bowl? You can do the same thing with leaves—iris and hosta leaves from your garden, snippets from your shrubs, and snitchings from your houseplants. Still not convinced that leaves are as good as flowers? Still not sure what to do with the greens you've got? At your next elegant sit-down for eight, try the arrangement pictured at the beginning of the chapter. In fact, I'll break my promise and tell you *how* to do this one. It's called an "asymmetrical" and works just as well with fresh flowers (the three cheap glads in Chapter 9 are done the same way—the candle takes the place of the first stem. And thank you, Mrs. Crawmer!).

The five basic stems (in this case, pale green sedum) go like so, each being three-quarters the length of the one before. Stem 4 goes to the back; stem 5 comes to the front. Superimpose five stems of a contrasting texture (here it's glossy, dark green *Euonymus patens*) cut slightly shorter. Fill in the base and back with still more varied greens (flashy white-striped variegated hosta and yellow-speckled aucuba). The variety of greens you can use is infinite—just remember to contrast your colors and textures, and try not to overstuff. To make your "all-green" look extra fresh and dewy, mist it with a flower atomizer just before company comes.

Greens you ought to have if you don't

Maybe you learned about azaleas at your mother's knee, but did your mother ever tell you about *osmanthus, enkianthus* and *aucuba?* Chances are she didn't know what they were, either. Nobody knows about osmanthus, enkianthus, and aucuba except garden clubbers and nurserymen. You could be looking at one in your garden right now and not know it.

As you might guess, osmanthus, enkianthus, and aucuba are three of the most invaluable, intriguing, and indispensable shrubs an arranger could have. Oddly enough, they're no harder to find, harder to grow, or harder on the pocketbook than ordinary run-of-the-mill shrubs—they're just harder to pronounce. That's why people don't dash out to buy them. Who wants to make a fool of herself at the nursery? On the other hand, who wants to make a career of horticultural nomenclature?

Here is a quick lesson in bushmanship—the lowdown on garden-club favorites with snooty-sounding names. Maybe the next time you go bush shopping, you won't come home with still another azalea. Maybe you'll even identify the "whatsis" in your backyard.

Most people walk right by *osmanthus*—they think it's just another holly bush. But touch it and you'll learn the difference. The glossy green leaves of osmanthus are softer and less prickly than holly, an obvious advantage when you're flower arranging. What's more, osmanthus has fragrant white flowers in the fall. *Enkianthus* has flowers in the spring, and you can take your pick of white, yellow, or red. It has handsome green leaves that turn brilliant colors in the fall (before they drop, incidentally—it's not an evergreen).

Andromeda (or *Pierus japonica*, if your nurseryman insists) is something like enkianthus, only better. It's an evergreen with graceful, drooping flowers that look like upside-down lilies of

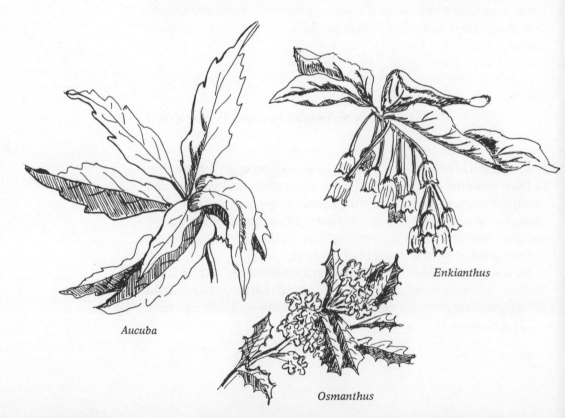

Aucuba

Enkianthus

Osmanthus

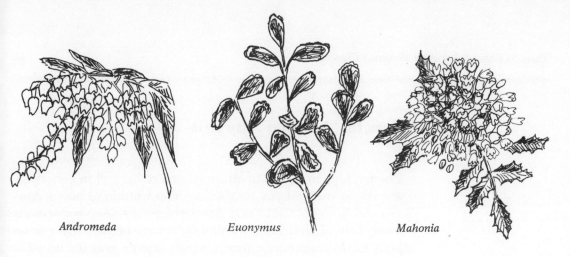

Andromeda   Euonymus   Mahonia

the valley. It's worth buying for the flowers alone, but it also has shiny, dark green leaves; sunny, almost-chartreuse leaves; and pale, rosy-copper leaves. What more could you ask?

Mahonia has even more tricks up its sleeve. Mahonia is another shrub that looks like holly (its other name is Oregon grape holly), but, in addition to green leaves, it has gold leaves and red leaves—all during the same season. In the spring it has bright yellow flowers, and in summer, deep blue "grapes."

Euonymus doesn't have to do anything but sit there. Its deep green leaves are as shiny as patent leather or, if you've forgotten what leather looks like, vinyl plastic. One variety of euonymus is actually called *Euonymus patens*. There's a variegated or silver-leaf euonymus, too, for a frosty-white touch in arrangements. There's also nonevergreen *Euonymus alatus*, famous with arrangers for its weird, corklike bark.

But if you could buy only one more bush before you die, or move to an apartment, the one bush to buy is *aucuba*. You don't even have to know what it looks like—just buy it. But do learn how to spell it and pronounce it. It's "a-kyew'bah," not "a-koo'bah," no matter what anyone tells you. Aucuba is the darling of the garden clubbers. Aucuba is a one-man flower show. Aucuba can make or break your career as a flower arranger—all-green or any other kind of arrangement. Actually, there are two kinds of aucuba. If you want the plain green, ask for *Aucuba japonica*; if you want green with yellow specks, ask for *Aucuba variegata*. If you want shiny red berries, be sure one of your aucubas is a male.

I could tell you about *nandina, pyracantha, cotoneaster, Magnolia stellata,* and *leucothoe,* but I don't want to drive you right back to the azalea counter. Look for these flower arrangers' pets at your favorite nursery; look for these and others in the glossary at the end of this chapter.

Greens for "have-not" city girls

Enough high-brow horticulture. If you're the girl in 24C, what is aucuba to you and you to aucuba? You wouldn't know a nandina bush if you fell into one. The only greens you ever see are growing behind plate-glass windows and have bright yellow price tags in spring, summer, winter, and fall. But even at the florist's, greens are cheaper than anemones. And even if you pay more than your country cousins, think of the money you save on mulches and manure.

What kind of greens will you find at the florist's? Asparagus fern, to be sure. Which you wouldn't take as a gift. But you might consider *leatherleaf fern*. It's the crisp, coarse, dark green variety currently favored in shops. It's not exciting but it's usable (provided it doesn't have ugly brown bumps on the back—that means it's been around too long). Need I mention *rhododendron leaves?* Is there anyone who doesn't know rhododendron leaves? If you're tired of rhododendron leaves, try *lemon* leaves (also called *salal* or *shallon*), *huckleberry* leaves, or *laurel* leaves. On the more exotic side, there are *ti* leaves, *loquat* leaves, *croton, lycopodium,* and assorted *palms*.

Two big favorites with garden clubbers are *Scotch broom* and *eucalyptus*. Not every florist will have them, but they're worth asking for. And by all means ask for *pittosporum* and *podocarpus*, even if you're never sure which is which. (Pittosporum is the one with leathery leaves and podocarpus the one with feathery spikes, or is it the other way around?)

Cheap as greens are, it's still smart to sniff out the cheapest greens in town. For run-of-the-mill greens, try any hole-in-the-wall cut-rate florist or supermarket that specializes in bargain-priced flowers. If you hit the right day, their greens may even be fresh. Or they may be so dirt-cheap that you'll be willing to compromise. For fancier greens, you'll probably have to go to a fancy-priced florist. But don't forget that, even in snooty flower shops, prices vary widely, if not wildly. Shop around. Sometimes the best florist in town is just as cheap as the street-corner vendor, and you can be sure his lemon leaves will last longer.

Is the florist's the only hunting ground for poor city girls? Not by a long shot. There's always the vegetable counter. Many a prize-winning arrangement has come straight from the lady's green-grocer. If garden clubbers use *parsley, beet greens,* and *cabbage leaves,* why not you? But that's another chapter altogether (namely, Fruit-and-Vegetable Bouquets).

City girls can also pick greens right at home—from their house-plants. Filching leaves from houseplants is an old garden-club trick. It won't hurt a flourishing philodendron or sansevieria a bit. For more on that subject, see Chapter 6.

Furthermore, city girls don't spend their entire lives buried up to their chins in concrete. They visit friends in suburbia and out in the country. They take vacation trips. They too can find greenery for free if they keep their eyes open. Even along the zoomingest freeway, there are treasures to be picked. Railroad tracks are especially fertile growing places for wildflowers and weeds. In fact, there's an astonishing amount of wild life right in the middle of most big cities—look in sidewalk cracks and in vacant lots. (See Chapter 3.) Obviously, greens on private property and in public parks are taboo. So is plant material that is

on the conservation list. Be sure to get a list of the protected plants in your state and let it, along with your conscience, be your guide.

Here are some for-instance arrangements for apartment dwellers:

• Rhododendron leaves, what else! But instead of tossing them into a bucket with your eyes closed, why not go a step further? Choose a boffo container, or thoughtfully prune the branches into an exciting design. Better still, play with lighting effects so that you have two leafy arrangements—one on the table and the other on the wall.

• Copy the centerpiece shown at the beginning of the chapter and described on page 11, substituting eucalyptus from the florist, leaves from your houseplants, and vegetable leaves from the supermarket for homegrown greens.

• Try a simple arrangement of purplish ti leaves, spiral eucalyptus, clusters of variegated pittosporum, and a few wisps of Scotch broom, as shown on the preceding page.

Poor girl's glossary of greens

You don't have to know *dracaena* from *dieffenbachia* to arrange greens, but it helps. Here is a list of the most common trees, shrubs, and plants. Common to garden clubbers, that is. To steer non–garden clubbers through the jungle, most greens have brief thumbnail descriptions. Others which are too common for words have, ergo, no descriptive words. Some *flowers* are included because of their leaves. Also vegetables, for the same reason.

In general, all garden-grown greens are listed under "Greens for Country Girls"; all store-bought greens are listed under "Greens for City Girls." But that doesn't mean that spade-and-trowelers can't buy ti leaves and cucumbers or that cliff-dwellers can't grow coleus. Use both lists. Also note that many houseplants on the city girls' list may also be grown outdoors in warm climates and are available at the florist's.

COUNTRY GIRLS

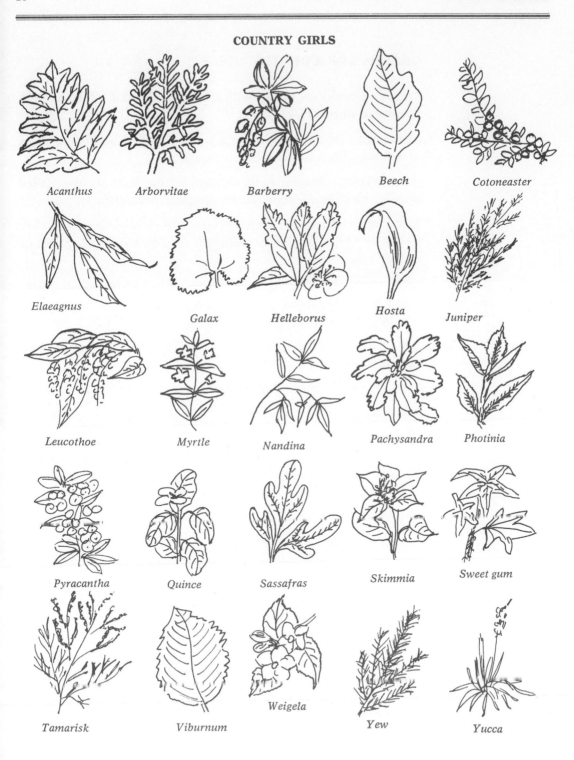

Acanthus   Arborvitae   Barberry   Beech   Cotoneaster

Elaeagnus   Galax   Helleborus   Hosta   Juniper

Leucothoe   Myrtle   Nandina   Pachysandra   Photinia

Pyracantha   Quince   Sassafras   Skimmia   Sweet gum

Tamarisk   Viburnum   Weigela   Yew   Yucca

GREENS FOR COUNTRY GIRLS

ABELIA   Deciduous shrub with clusters of small white or pink flowers in summer.

ACANTHUS   Perennial with large notched leaves and white, rose, or lavender flower spikes in late summer.

AMARANTHUS   Annual with red and bronze foliage; also called love-lies-bleeding, Joseph's coat, summer poinsettia.

AMPELOPSIS   Vigorous, unfussy vine with large leaves and clusters of berries that change color; also called monkshood-vine or pepper vine.

ANDROMEDA   Near-perfect evergreen shrub with glossy, bright green leaves, pinkish-bronze new growth, and white spring flowers that resemble lilies of the valley.

AQUILEGIA   Perennial with distinctive flowers and fernlike foliage; also called columbine.

ARBORVITAE   Evergreen with fanlike sprays of scalelike leaves.

ARTEMISIA   Perennial with handsome white, gray or silvery foliage; sometimes called dusty miller or mountain sage.

AUCUBA   Evergreen shrub with notched, bright green leaves (*A. japonica*) or yellow-flecked leaves (*A. variegata*) and bright red fruits in fall.

AZALEA

BARBERRY   Deciduous or evergreen shrub with small leaves brightly colored in fall, yellow flowers and black or red fruits.

BIRD'S-NEST FERN   Fern with individual three-foot fronds in bird's-nestlike clumps; also with fine, feathery two-foot fronds.

BASIL   Annual with pungent leaves; also an ornamental purple-leaved variety that tends to reseed.

BEECH   Large deciduous tree with gray bark and dark green, copper, golden, or purple foliage.

BOSTON IVY

BOXWOOD

CANNA Tuberous plant with distinctive tall leaves as well as showy summer flowers.

CASTOR-OIL PLANT Easy-to-grow annual with big, beautiful bronze, green, or dark maroon leaves.

CEDAR

CLEMATIS Vine with deciduous or evergreen leaves and handsome flowers in many colors.

COLEUS Annual plant grown for its colorful leaves of pink-green, white-green, etc.

COTONEASTER Favorite deciduous or evergreen shrub with distinctive small leaves; many choice varieties.

DICENTRA Perennial with fernlike foliage; also called bleeding heart.

ECHEVERIA Succulent plant with rosette-shaped leaves; also called hen-and-chickens. Can be grown indoors or out. Cut rosettes *may* be available through big-city florists.

ELAEAGNUS Shrub or tree with ornamental silvery foliage; also called Russian olive.

ENKIANTHUS Deciduous shrub with fine foliage that turns brilliant colors in fall; has white, red, or yellow flowers in spring.

EUONYMUS Evergreen shrub with handsome, patent-leathery leaves—dark green, white and green, or yellow and green.

FORSYTHIA

GALAX Perennial evergreen wildflower with glossy, leathery round leaves that last up to two months (widely available at florists', too).

HELLEBORUS Evergreen perennial with distinctive notched leaves and winter blooms; also called Christmas rose.

HOLLY (Ilex)

HOSTA Perennial plant with sturdy large curling leaves in solid green, blue-green, and green and white.

HYDRANGEA

ILEX (Holly)

IRIS

ISMENE Bulbous plant with summer-blooming lilylike flowers and yellow-green spearlike leaves that stay green all summer.

IVY

JUNIPER

KOLKWITZIA Easy-to-grow deciduous shrub with attractive gray-green leaves with a hairy texture, and profuse pink flowers in June; also called beauty bush.

LAUREL

LAUREL CHERRY Evergreen shrub with glossy leaves and white flowers in spikes. Also called cherry laurel.

LEUCOTHOE Evergreen shrub with handsome pointed leathery leaves that change color with the seasons, and lily of the valley–like flowers.

LIGUSTRUM (Privet)

LOQUAT Evergreen tree with rough-textured leaf rosettes, fragrant white flowers, and edible plum-shaped yellow fruit.

MAGNOLIA

MAGNOLIA STELLATA Deciduous shrub with early spring flowers followed by dense yellow-green foliage and "pussy willows" in the winter. Also called star magnolia.

MAIDENHAIR FERN Lovely, delicate favorite with more or less fan-shaped leaf segments and black stems.

MAHONIA Evergreen shrub with hollylike leaves that turn bronze-red in fall, yellow spring flowers, and blue summer "grapes." Also called Oregon grape holly.

MANZANITA Evergreen West Coast shrub with purplish bark, interesting branches.

MAPLE

MYRTLE Evergreen shrub with aromatic glossy leaves.

NANDINA Evergreen shrub with canelike stems and lovely lacy foliage that turns brilliant colors in fall; has white flower clusters followed by red berries. Also called heavenly bamboo.

NASTURTIUM

OAK

OSMANTHUS   Evergreen shrub or tree with glossy foliage like dainty, supple holly leaves. Also called sweet olive.

PACHYSANDRA   Evergreen ground cover with attractive toothed leaves in rosettes on short stems.

PARSLEY

PEACH

PEAR

PEONY

PHOTINIA   Deciduous or evergreen shrub with colorful foliage, white flowers, and red fruit.

PLUM

PYRACANTHA   Evergreen shrub with shiny, dark green leaves, spiny branches, white spring flowers; grown mostly for its fiery red or orange berries. Also called firethorn.

QUINCE

RHODODENDRON

SAGE

SASSAFRAS   Deciduous tree with leaves of several mittenlike shapes that turn brilliant red in fall.

SCOTCH BROOM   Evergreen shrub with spring flowers and distinctive green stems and twigs all year.

SEDUM   Succulent plant of many different sizes and shapes, mostly cactuslike.

SKIMMIA   Evergreen with fragrant flowers, red berries, and attractive leathery, fleshy leaves in yellow-green.

SNOW-ON-THE-MOUNTAIN   Annual with white-margined leaves and white flowers. Also called euphorbia.

SPRUCE

SWEET CICELY   Perennial herb with fragrant fernlike leaves.

SWEET GUM   Deciduous tree with handsome star-shaped leaves that turn brilliant red in fall.

TAMARISK   Deciduous shrub with small heatherlike gray-green leaves as delicate and feathery as the flowers.

VIBURNUM

WEIGELA   Deciduous shrub with bell-shaped flowers; variegated types have green and white or yellow and white leaves.

YEW (Taxus)

YUCCA   Evergreen plant with tough sword-shaped leaves in rosettes and with clusters of white flowers.

GREENS FOR CITY GIRLS

AMARYLLIS   Bulbous plant with enormous lilylike flowers and three-foot-tall leaves.

ARTICHOKE

ASPIDISTRA   Evergreen with shiny large leathery leaves; tough and neglectable. Also called cast-iron plant.

BEET

BEGONIA

CABBAGE

CACTUS

CALADIUM   Tuberous plant with brightly colored heart-shaped leaves in red-green, white-green, or red-white.

CAMELLIA

CARROT

CELERY

CHINESE EVERGREEN   Houseplant with long green or variegated leaves; grows in water.

CHLOROPHYTUM   Houseplant with slender leaves marked with white or yellow. New plants form at the ends of long racemes. Also called spider plant.

CITY GIRLS

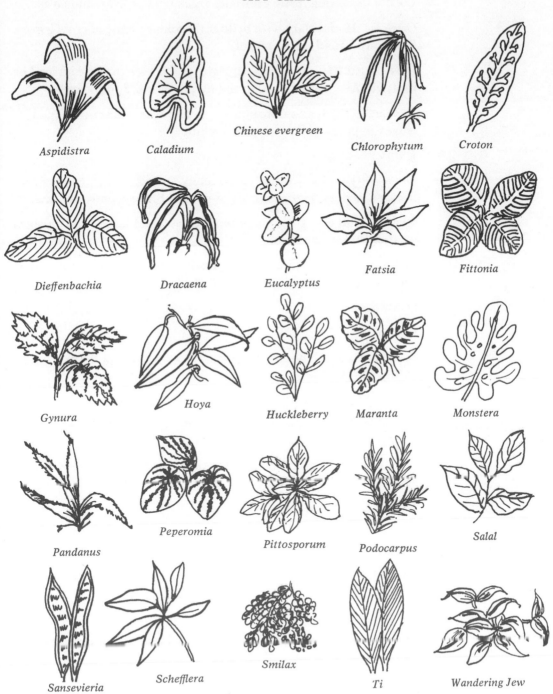

Aspidistra

Caladium

Chinese evergreen

Chlorophytum

Croton

Dieffenbachia

Dracaena

Eucalyptus

Fatsia

Fittonia

Gynura

Hoya

Huckleberry

Maranta

Monstera

Pandanus

Peperomia

Pittosporum

Podocarpus

Salal

Sansevieria

Schefflera

Smilax

Ti

Wandering Jew

Cocculus   Long-lasting florist's green with shiny oval leaves.

Croton   Houseplant with brilliantly colored long, narrow leaves. Some are broad, some spiral.

Dieffenbachia   Has large upright oval leaves that are striped or mottled. Also called mother-in-law plant and dumb cane.

Dracaena   Tall palmlike plant with handsome narrow striped leaves in green-yellow or green-white.

Endive

Eucalyptus   California tree of many species, the most common florist's variety having spirals of unique blue-green round leaves.

Fatsia   Tall evergreen plant with large lobed leaves and clusters of small white flowers.

Fittonia   Houseplant with handsome heart-shaped leaves that are veined red or white.

Gardenia

Geranium

Ginger   Houseplant with fine, glossy leaves and showy multicolored flowers.

Grape Ivy   Vine with fast-growing glossy leaves.

Gynura   Houseplant with leaves and stems covered with velvety purple hairs, orange flowers. Also called velvet plant.

Holly Fern   Hardy fern with shaggy stalks and glossy leaves somewhat like holly leaves.

Hoya   Evergreen vine with shiny green foliage and fragrant flowers. Also called wax plant.

Huckleberry

Lycopodium   Florist's evergreen foliage with feathery needles.

Maranta   Has interesting spotted varicolored leaves; closes up at night. Also called prayer plant.

Monstera   Big evergreen climber with huge leaves, deeply lobed and perforated, and calla lilylike flowers.

Norfolk Island Pine   Small, symmetrical evergreen tree with neatly tiered branches.

OXALIS   Bulbous plant with cloverlike leaves and flowers.

PALM

PALMETTO

PANDANUS   Has long spiny-edged, white- or yellow-banded leaves. Also called screw pine.

PARSLEY

PEPEROMIA   Houseplant with silver- or cream-marked heart-shaped leaves; sometimes called watermelon begonia.

PHILODENDRON

PITTOSPORUM   Evergreen with clusters of handsome leathery oval leaves, white flowers and berries.

PODOCARPUS   Evergreen with feathery, palmlike branches of narrow, dense leaves.

RHUBARB

RUBBER PLANT

SALAL   Pacific coast shrub with glossy dark leaves. Also called shallon and lemon leaves.

SANSEVIERIA   Upright foliage plant with thick swordlike leaves striped or banded yellow or light green. Also called snake plant.

SCHEFFLERA   Tall houseplant with umbrella-shaped leaf clusters and red flower spikes. Also called umbrella plant.

SMILAX   Perennial vine with oval-shaped leaves (botanically, *Asparagus asparagoides*).

SPINACH

STRELITZIA   Subtropical perennial with distinctive leaves and spectacular blue and orange flowers. Also called bird-of-paradise.

TI   Exotic palm leaves with purplish tinge. (Pronounced "tea.")

WANDERING JEW   Houseplant with trailing stems of reddish-purple or green leaves with stripes.

2
Fruit-and-Vegetable
Bouquets

IN EUROPE you don't just look at the centerpiece—you eat it. A bowl of fresh fruit is as tony a table arrangement as you can get. (In Ireland, when Mrs. Murphy is putting on airs, they say, "Fruit on the table and nobody sick in the house.") Why do we Americans think fruits and vegetables belong in the kitchen? Fruits and vegetables have been party decorations since early Greek and Roman bashes, and the greengrocer may be the best florist you ever had.

The minute you say fruits and vegetables, everyone thinks of Thanksgiving, right? Well, bountiful harvest cornucopias *are* beautiful, but who needs another description of apples, grapes, and gourds tumbling over the table? How about using the old favorites in fresh new ways? Have you ever tried a pyramid of frosty green limes in the summer? Have you ever scooped out a satiny purple eggplant for a vase? Have you ever heard of a bride throwing a cabbage bouquet?

More than that, how about using fruits and vegetables you've never dreamed of arranging? Asparagus spears, for instance. Also

27

mushrooms, rhubarb, radishes, onions, beets, Brussels sprouts, and cranberries. I can see you squirming now. Obviously, we're getting into the kind of kooky, arty arrangements you hate. Asparagus spears? Rhubarb? Next I'll be telling you to scrub up your potatoes. Right. But fruit-and-vegetable arranging can also be as simple and natural as you like. I remember my first inside peek at the world of garden clubbers. The occasion was a Christmas party at the home of the club president, and you can believe that the lady's house was decorated to the nines. I'd never seen such magnificent garlands, swags, wreaths, and table arrangements! But do you know the one thing I remember now, years later? A simple silver bowl of polished apples on the sideboard.

Fruits without frills

I still think a bowl of shiny, blushing-red apples is the poshest winter arrangement going. In the summer I switch to lemons and limes. Clever and original? Hardly. But try it and see if eyes don't pop (remember, this is fruit-in-the-kitchen land). You can "arrange" your fruit or pile it willy-nilly. If you're appalled at how many lemons and limes it takes for even a casual heaping, cheat with a bed of chicken wire or a bottom layer of grapefruits in your bowl. For a classical pyramid, alternate rows of limes and lemons on a crystal dish or bed of greens, with or without a few green sprigs tucked between the fruit. Use the larger fruits at the bottom, and spear each layer to the next with rounded toothpicks.

Have you ever thought of one grapefruit as a flower arrangement? Simply upend a footed goblet and perch one perfect golden "globe" on top (a little florist's clay will help keep it in place). Terrific on a stark see-through lucite table. If your decor is more Williamsburg than with-it, use a fancier glass and add a base of glossy greenery or a few trailing tendrils of ivy. Try a whole grouping of fruits on assorted goblets, some upended, some right side up, on top of a mirror. Intersperse squatty candles on some goblets, and garnish with greens. You can also pile fruits into any large glass container—hurricane lamp, outsized brandy snifter, or even a fish bowl.

Almost any fruit or vegetable can stand on its own, once you start seeing it with an arranger's eye. If you don't have red roses,

fill a basket with jumbo California strawberries or ripe red tomatoes. If you don't have white daisies, try a bowl of snow-white mushrooms or cauliflower florets. And who needs costly greens from the florist? You've got cabbage leaves, celery stalks, asparagus spears, green peppers, artichokes, parsley, curly kale, spinach, chard, and watercress to choose from. Just the lettuce family alone can keep you in flower-arranging greens the year round. Choose from iceberg, Boston, romaine, Bibb, chicory, curly endive, Cos, escarole, and bronze-leaf. Then there are dozens of interesting herbs—mint, thyme, sage, dill, rosemary, oregano, rue, coriander, and chives. I'm not sure that herbs belong under fruits and vegetables, but I'm sure they belong in your flower containers. The next time you're in Williamsburg, notice the lux-uriant all-green bouquets in the Restoration kitchens. They're mostly common herbs.

The mixed-vegetable bouquet

So much for all-of-a-kind and one-fruit arrangements. On to bigger and better things. Do you need a last-minute arrangement for unexpected dinner guests? You can probably pull one right out of your refrigerator. Here's one that won a blue ribbon for the arranger at a Garden Club of America show. The ingredients? Hot peppers, pearl onions, Brussels sprouts, apples, squash, a pineapple. (Robert Webb of New York is famous for such.)

You'll find whole books full of fruit-and-vegetable ideas, but if you want to be a little different, go monochromatic. How about a cool, sophisticated all-green arrangement? Use pears, limes, green grapes, green apples, green bananas, cucumbers, green peppers, zucchini, green beans, or peas in their pods. Add any of the leafy green vegetables already listed or fresh garden foliage and, if you want to go all out, green Envy zinnias, bells of Ireland, or echeveria rosettes.

For a sunny all-gold arrangement, use yellow wax beans, squashes, pale pumpkins, grapefruit, lemons, oranges, or ripe bananas—with or without bright yellow or orange flowers and yellow-green leaves. Reds and purples are even more dramatic. Try cherries, eggplant, plums, Tokay grapes, red onions, blue kale, purple-capped turnips, and red cabbage. (Half a red cabbage is more interesting than a whole one. In fact, halved red cabbages mounted on sticks make fantastic fake flowers.)

The cabbage arrangement at the beginning of the chapter took five minutes to make and cost a hair over one dollar. It contains two purple cabbage heads (58¢ for both), seven peaches (48¢), three radishes (two bunches for 35¢), and one spray of wild staghorn sumac (city girls can use red grapes just as well). When sumac is picked in early August, the fruit is still partly green and partly burnished, coppery red. Purple, red and peach are a nifty color combination, and, if you're flush, tuck in a few peach-colored petunias or gladiolus florets. The "container" is a lucite kitchen cutting board set on a silver cake stand. You don't need the stand, and an ordinary wooden breadboard would do. So would a polished burl, gleaming mirror, or slab of purple-toned slate. You don't need the spikey, pale green angel trumpet pods, either—I added them simply because they were sitting on the kitchen counter at the time.

Have you ever seen an asparagus "vase"? It's too fussy an operation for me. You stand the spears on end and pin them, fence-style, all around a cardboard bucket. I'd rather see them waving in the breeze along with a few fresh daffodils. Could anything be more symbolic of spring? Here's 19¢ worth of asparagus (all the funny-looking ones that nobody else wanted) in an ordinary lamp globe with a drinking-glass insert for the flowers.

Or try leafy celery stalks with gay marigolds. Dark green clumps of curly parsley are a perfect foil for bright red strawberries, and satiny green peppers go beautifully with roses or mums. All you need for a container is an old-fashioned berry bas-

ket, if you can find one in this day of tacky green plastic. New York florist Robert Miglio updates the old cornucopia by heaping an antique market basket with cabbage, broccoli, artichokes, and apples and tucking in two Oasis-filled flower pots of vivid garden flowers.

Clever garden clubbers can turn a hand of bananas into an elegant crescent arrangement. Or they'll line up five pears in a subtle "abstract" (point the stems in different directions, please). But you don't have to work that hard. Add leaves snitched from a houseplant to a handful of oranges on a footed compote. Simple bowls of oranges are very big in the fancy decorating magazines. Add ivy and sprigs of lavender ageratum to a bowl of red and purple plums. Tuck just a few yellow zinnias in with your lemons, or a few salmon-pink petunias in with your peaches. A bunch of grapes is an arrangement all by itself, but you can gild the lily by frosting the grapes and adding glossy green foliage.

When you're really in a hurry, there's nothing like driftwood. I've seen everything from potatoes to spring onions sitting on driftwood in prize-winning arrangements. Another natural and time-saving partner for fruits and vegetables is dried material. Clouds of waving grains or grasses, dried magnolia leaves, or clusters of gay strawflowers will do the trick. Florist John Noblitt piles red and green peppers in a basket with pinecones.

I love it; what is it?

So far we've been talking about good, honest fruits and vegetables, like spinach, that am what they am and don't try to be anything else. Now let's have some fun. Believe me, you can have more fun with plain old produce than you've ever had with florist's flowers. Once you stop thinking about your stomach and start thinking about arranging, your journeys through the supermarket will be as thrilling as a trip to the Philadelphia Flower Show.

What do asparagus tips look like? Dainty grape hyacinth buds, of course. What does a crookneck squash look like? An abstract bird any sculptor would be proud of. Everyone knows that the creamy white florets of cauliflower and Brussels sprouts are as pretty as sweetheart roses, but have you ever noticed the blue-green velvet blossoms of broccoli?

Collard greens may not be every Yankee's favorite dish, but what more could an arranger ask for? They look for all the world like exotic green and white houseplant leaves, and they're even sold by the leaf (well, actually, by the pound, but you're free to forage through the bin of leaves for the most exciting shapes and colors). Squashes in odd colors and shapes have always been good decorating bets, but have you ever seen a pattypan squash on a stick? It looks like a big white modern flower (try the small greenish ones, too). Pot them in a gleaming, deep purple eggplant along with black radish roses and a flowery slice of magenta-red cabbage. *Quel chic.* Or plant just one pattypan in a sand-filled throwaway plastic glass with a red radish for a center and a wired-on cabbage leaf. Unless you need them for tomorrow's dinner, they're twice as glossy with a coat of clear plastic spray. You can poke the dowels right into your eggplant, but it's less garbagey if you scoop it out and fill it with wet sand.

For little white modern flowers, stick cream-of-the-crop mushroom caps on toothpicks or wire stems. Cranberries can be wired into jewel-like flower clusters; tiny onions or potatoes can be wired into grapelike clusters. Staple beet or rhubarb leaves together and what have you got? A magnificent, giant red peony. Poke crisp carrot curls into a quartered red cabbage and it's a cactus-type zinnia, spider mum, or you-name-it. In a pinch, use cucumber spears for leaves.

Garden clubbers turn cucumbers into "water lilies" and other exotic flowers (these are a little tricky, so be sure your cukes are underripe). They turn bean pods into modern spirals by twisting them around a pencil. Thin slices of turnip can be curled into "calla lilies" with brown toothpick stamens. In fact, you can even use paper flower patterns with really thin, crisp slices of turnips, beets, or carrots. Corn husks can be doubled into flower-like petals with a gilded ear of corn for the center. Green pepper "tulips" are cinchy—slice off the top, cut V-shaped scallops, and mount on a dowel. By now you should be popping with your own ideas, but here's one last goodie—a vegetable "tussy-mussy," yet. For *your* nosegay, use radish roses, cauliflower florets, broccoli blossoms, and fringed carrot slices on toothpicks. Poke into styrofoam; add green kurly kale and a paper doily.

Exotica, et cetera

With so many garden-variety groceries to play with, you never have to leave your own pea patch. But there's a whole world of oddball edibles in gourmet shops and big-city markets for the adventurous arranger. I've even found weirdies right around the corner (in the same blessed supermarket that keeps me in cut-rate cut flowers).

Black radishes, for instance, like the ones you saw teamed with pattypan squash. That's right, black—and some grow as big as baseballs. There are also white radishes, which are long and skinny. There are Italian eggplants, a boon to arrangers because they're shiny, purple, and *small*. There are Cuban peppers, striped red and green. There are shallots, okra, leek, celery knobs, ginger, root parsley, and horseradish—not unfamiliar to gourmet cooks but not found in every produce department. Among the offbeat fruits are red bananas, green bananas, and plantains (jumbo green "bananas" for baking or frying). There are mangoes, kumquats, papayas, papaws, persimmons, and prickly pears. Besides the usual cantaloupes, honeydews, and watermelons, look for Persians, Crenshaws, and casabas.

In a big-city fruit market, you might luck into sugar cane or carambola ("star fruit" from Florida). Wrinkly, chartreuse-skinned osage oranges will last for weeks without drying up or decaying. Reddish, cubical pomegranates are another good buy—they can be dried and kept indefinitely (just place on a rack in a dark, dry place for two or three months). You can enjoy red onions and hot peppers while they're drying—just string them up in your kitchen or tie them wreath-style to a bent coat hanger. For a Christmas wreath you won't want to take down, fasten red chili peppers, plastic-wrapped garlic bulbs, nutmegs and nuts, sprigs of rosemary, and dried parsley or bay leaves to a styrofoam base.

Artichokes are an old garden-club favorite, fresh or dry. To dry them, hang them upside down in a dark, dry place for a month or so; stuff Kleenex between the petals if you want an open rosette. And have you ever seen a Jerusalem artichoke? It's not an artichoke (which is the fleshy base of an herb) at all but the tuber of a sunflower. And that's what it looks like—a knobby, dried-up old brown rhizome. Anyway, it will keep your friends guessing. (It has nothing to do with Jerusalem, either—it got its name, by mistake, from the Italian word for sunflower, *girasole*—if you follow me, or even care to.)

The garden of oddballs

If you can't find gourmet produce in stores, you can always grow your own. You'll probably have to grow kohlrabi in any event. It's so freaky-looking that nobody sells it, but garden club-bers love it (it looks something like an octopus, and to add to the sport, it's also called rape plant). Another offbeat vegetable, salsify, is also called oyster plant—not because it looks like an oyster but because it tastes like one. Aside from the edible root, it has (and I quote) "peduncled heads of purplish flowers."

Look for seed packs of borecole, a dwarf blue curly kale. Look for India mustard, which has giant curly green leaves like endive. In case you're confused about ordinary green endive and fancy white Belgian endive, I asked the clerk how come they both have the same name. He said they don't—one is "en-dive" and the other is "ahn-deev." Oh, well, the truth is that they're both types of chicory, and "ahn-deev" is purposely blanched white be-fore marketing.

Look for edible-pod peas such as "Dwarf Gray Sugar," with red flowers that look like sweet peas. New "Chipman's Canada Red" rhubarb has extra-red stems and extra-pretty creamy flow-ers. "Dark Opal" basil is mahogany-colored. And ornamental (or flowering) kale and cabbage couldn't be more so! One sensa-tional plant is all you need for an instant centerpiece that will knock guests dead. You'll find pink, rose, purple, white, and cream. Note that color changes don't occur until cool weather, but here in Maryland the blooms last into January! Write Way-side or Park for seed (neighbors, dash to Valley View Farms, Cockeysville).

How about growing other old standbys in crazy colors? You'll find pink, yellow, or orange tomatoes, bright red "Ruby" lettuce,

"White Wonder" cucumbers, deep purple "Royalty" string beans (don't worry, they turn green when cooked), and golden-orange "Gold Nugget" beets.

If your decorating tastes are really far out, try Northrup's "Silly Seeds" or Fredonia's "Fun-Tastic" seeds. Yard-long beans, giant five-pound round white Shogoin radishes, nine-inch-long Sakurajima radishes, chop-suey greens, and serpentine green "snake cucumbers" are a few of the zany seeds on the shelves.

Please don't eat the bowl

Who needs fancy flower containers when there are fruits and vegetables around? A shiny red apple filled with daisies or mums at each place setting is one of the quickest tricks I know (you'll see one on page 120). Or you can use a center bowl of apples and scatter the miniature apple bouquets at random around it. At Christmas, stuff your apples with sprigs of shiny green holly. Or fill plump oranges with curly green parsley and tiny cherry tomatoes. Flowers can be poked right into an apple, but it's best to scoop out oranges and add a vial of water.

Pumpkins, coconuts, gourds, and squashes are natural containers for flowers or other decorative fruits and vegetables. Look for gaudy-hued Turk's-cap squash. Try hollowing out the center of a gourd and standing it on end, or use it as a hanging container. One of the handsomest "vases" I've seen was a scooped-out purple eggplant heaped with purple, red, and pink anemones. Use half a leafy pineapple sliced lengthwise or half a Persian melon. Or how about a trio of scalloped grapefruit "bowls" on a bed of greens?

Of course, fruits make good containers for dessert fruits, too. I'm sure you've been carving out watermelon "boats" for years and have your own pet version, but here's an ultra-elegant watermelon basket designed by a famous chef.

To make a watermelon basket, take a slice off the end of a large melon and stand it upright. To fashion the handle, make two parallel cuts 1½" apart, cutting from the narrow end to the the center. Remove the two side sections, leaving the center slice attached for a handle. Score the melon as indicated, then remove the center meat with a large melon-ball cutter. Scoop out the pulp from the top of the rind at ¾" intervals. Fill the basket with sweetened mixed fruits and berries. Fill the holes in the top of the rind with cantaloupe balls, and garnish the top with rings of honeydew balls, overlapping slices of strawberries and grapefruit and orange sections.

How about a meant-to-be-eaten vegetable decoration? Instead of poking cocktail shrimp into a prosaic head of lettuce, pick out an enormous head of red or green cabbage (ornamental kale is even better, as I've mentioned). Soak the cabbage in ice water and unfold the outer petals into a giant rose. Take a slice off the base so it sits at a glamorous angle, and fill the center with plump pink shrimp on toothpicks. Garnish with radish "roses" and flickering candles. (For extra-fancy roses, cut staggered diagonal slits in jumbo-size radishes; insert paper-thin slices cut from other smaller radishes.)

Happiness is an "apple tree"

I've noticed that all respectable flower-arranging books include a chapter on Christmas decorations. I'll skip the usual Romanesque garlands of fruit, Della Robbia wreaths, and grapy things in exquisite eighteenth-century epergnes—not because they're too hard but because they're too easy. All you really need is a good picture to copy (you'll find them in dozens of books), a few Simple-Simon mechanics (you'll find them at the end of this chapter), and plenty of time (that you'll have to find for yourself). As far as I'm concerned, you need only one Christmas decoration—a Williamsburg "apple tree."

Have you ever seen a bona fide apple-tree stand? It's the best and funniest-looking Christmas present I've ever received. To look at the "before," you'd never dream of the glorious "after." It's simply a cone of solid wood mounted on a base, with nails sticking out at precise intervals. Unfortunately, you can't buy one for money, only love. But if you don't happen to have a good friend and neighbor who happens to be a nut on Colonial Williamsburg, happens to dabble in carpentry, and happens to remember chance cocktail-party remarks, you can make do with

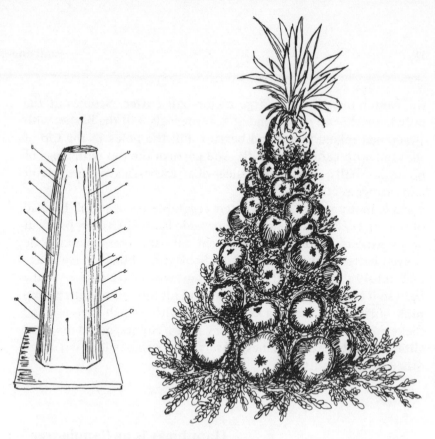

a styrofoam cone. Instead of impaling your fruit on nails, attach it to the form with toothpicks.

Like most fruit decorations, apple trees aren't hard, just time-consuming. You can't start on Christmas Eve. My particular stand has thirty-six nails, and just picking out thirty-six perfect apples at the market is a day's work. Remember that you need small, middling, and jumbo-size apples—plus tiny "lady apples" for the top, which nine out of ten markets don't sell. Then you have to polish your thirty-six apples. But once that's done, the rest is a cinch. Simply impale the apples on the nails, stuff well-soaked boxwood in between, and crown your masterpiece with a lush-leaved pineapple, ancient symbol of hospitality.

Instead of apples, you can use lemons, limes, and pears. If the fruits are too nearly the same size, halve or three-quarter some of them and hide your surgery with boxwood. An occasional squirt with a flower mister will help keep your boxwood dewy, if you don't mind reshining your apples. In case you attempt your own bona fide stand, use rustproof finishing nails or you'll have rusty apple pie. (Poor girls can't afford to throw out thirty-six perfect apples.)

If apples and pears are too, too humdrum for you, put cabbages, onions, leeks, artichokes, and peas on your tree. That's what florist George Cothran did for the Skitch Hendersons one Christmas. I don't know the price, but I'll bet it would keep you and me in coleslaw for the rest of our days.

Tossed salad of arranging tips

- Use underripe produce whenever possible.
- Preserve and polish produce with one or two coats of clear plastic spray (unless you plan to eat it).
- Soak cabbage, kale, and chard in cold water for several hours after removing from your vegetable crisper, to remove odor. Some experts recommend a coat of plastic spray.
- Remove a bottom slice from fruit and vegetable "containers" to level them.
- Insert jelly jars or plastic bowls into scooped-out "containers" to hold water and flowers.
- Use toothpicks to anchor together fruits and vegetables in an arrangement.
- Use water picks or plastic pill bottles to keep flowers fresh.
- Poke flowers right into juicy fruits and vegetables; the juice will keep them fresh for a day or two, at least.
- Dip sliced ends of fruits and vegetables in melted paraffin to seal in the juices.
- Lemons, limes, and oranges will dry naturally in about a month. Don't touch them, though, or they'll mold. (And don't worry, they go through a "soft" stage first.)
- To frost fruits, dip into foamy beaten egg whites, then granulated sugar. Dry on waxed paper.
- Protect silver bowls with a lining of foil.
- Clean fruit with wax paper.
- Rub a little lipstick or colored chalk onto green pears or yellow peaches to give a rosy glow.

3

Wild and Wonderful

WHEN GARDEN CLUBBERS SWEAR that the best things in life are free, when flower arrangers win ribbons with skunk cabbage, when the garden editor of the *New York Sunday Times* writes an "ode to a chickweed"—it must mean something. What it means is that weeds are "in," and all your troubles are over.

Garden clubbers, of course, have always loved weeds and wildflowers. It's how they one-up the hoi polloi. Any dodo can flower-arrange with pretty garden flowers. Any yo-yo can buy a bird-of-paradise at the florist's. But only a garden clubber can spot milkweed pods at fifty-five miles an hour on the Jersey Turnpike.

Get to know weeds and wildlings and you'll have more "flowers" than you know what to do with. Luckily, for all their newly acquired chic, the price hasn't jumped one bit. They're still scot-free. The only thing you have to remember is that many wildflowers are now on state-protected lists and mustn't be picked. But there are still many more okay-to-pick weeds than not-okay (you'll find a list further on).

Fair warning: flower arranging with weeds may rearrange

your whole life. Do you always look straight ahead when walking on a city street? Do you nod and doze on long, monotonous thruway trips? Do the starts-and-stops and unexplained delays on the commuter train drive you wild? Once you discover the treasures in the wild brown yonder, you'll be glued to every sidewalk crack, every mile of gray stuff along the highways, and every boring stretch of railroad track. You'll almost pray (very quietly) for the family car to break down.

But don't let any sourgrass grow under your feet. Weeds are "in"er than ever these back-to-nature days. You'll have to get there ahead of not only the garden clubbers and bulldozers but also the Euell Gibbons bunch, out foraging for dinner. City girls especially had better beat a path to their vacant lots. Would you believe that on a cold winter day in downtown Detroit one sharp-eyed scavenger found eleven different wild edibles under the snow? Euell himself once found twenty-five varieties of "free foods" within a hundred feet of a supermarket. "If you can't beat 'em, eat 'em," says a Nebraska professor turned nature-boy. "If you can't lick 'em, pick 'em," say I.

"Miss America" weeds

By weeds I mean anything that grows wild and free—flowers, leaves, grasses, branches, pods. But let's start with the "glamor" weeds that don't look like weeds. Everybody knows and loves bright white field daisies, black-eyed Susans, violets, and buttercups. Why don't more people bring them home to arrange, just like florist's daisies, violets, and ranunculus (the same family as buttercups)? Chances are, you've been scared off by dozens of loving little limp bouquets brought home in your children's hot little hands. You've just assumed that field flowers won't live in the house. Nonsense. Aside from a few prima donnas and a few cases where picking a flower will kill the whole plant, cut wildflowers will last as long as most cut garden flowers. Most pros keep a bucket of water in the car or at least a supply of wet newspapers in plastic bags. But some flowers are amazingly resilient. I once carted a bunch of daisy fleabane from morning to evening in a hot, windy car (we were on our way home from vacation, and all my plastic bags were filled up). After a few hours' bath in a motel basin, they looked as fresh and perky as ever. (P.S.: Of course you can have fresh flowers every night in your motel room. Some of my best bouquets have been Howard Johnson's weeds. And never stay in the car while your husband's fueling up—gas-station weeds are gorgeous.)

One of the best keepers, thank heavens, is Queen Anne's lace. It's actually just a wild carrot, but many arrangers think Queen Anne's lace is the most exquisite flower that grows. You probably would too if you had to buy it by the stem from a florist. Fresh or dried, alone or with other flowers, arranged in a silver epergne or on a hunk of driftwood, the elegant "snowflake flower" is hard to beat.

How about good old goldenrod? Just as with Queen Anne's lace, there's so much of it around that nobody looks at it twice. Goldenrod is a spectacular flower (or flowers—there are several different kinds). It can hold its own against any yellow bloom in your garden, and it's not so deadly as some scaredy cats think. Naturally, you wouldn't wave it under your allergic daughter's poor red nose, but a few sprays in the average household won't hurt a bit. If you're still jittery, keep your goldenrod outside. It's magnificent in basket bouquets on the front door (with Queen Anne's lace, of course, and a few gaudy zinnias). Or hang it up to dry—it's absolutely sneeze-proof in dried arrangements.

"Unknowns" you should know

So much for beginners' weeds. If you never get beyond golden-rod, you're still ahead of the game. But there's a whole wide world of wildlings out there. There's *Joe-pye weed*, worth loving for the name alone (they say it was named for an old Indian medicine man). Joe-pye doesn't grow just anywhere and every-where, but at least you can't miss it when it's there. It grows as high as twelve feet and has huge clusters of pink or red flowers on top. I've seen it in open meadows as well as dense woods. *Mullein* is another giant. It's the weird-looking weed with a clus-ter of velvety leaves on the ground and a six-foot spike in the

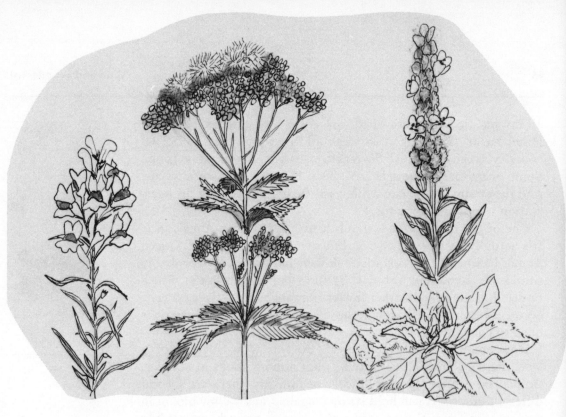

Butter-and-eggs   *Joe-pye weed*   *Mullein*

middle. You and I wouldn't call it pretty, but garden clubbers
hunt it down like bloodhounds. They use the silver-green rosettes
like flowers and always have a bunch of stalks drying in the
garage. The best place to look for mullein is by the railroad tracks.
In fact, railroad beds are good hunting grounds for many weeds.
Look there for *butter-and-eggs* (with yellow snapdragon-type
flowers on two-foot spikes), wild *evening primrose* (with flat yellow flowers like buttercups), and tall, spiky, magenta-flowered
lythrum. Try burned-over areas at the dump for *wild coreopsis,
wild geranium, Deptford pink, knapweed,* and *steeple bush.*

Another common wayside wanderer is *bouncing bet* (or soap-
wort). It looks something like phlox, only shorter, and has paler
leaves than garden phlox. *Wild mustard* is marvelous. It's loaded
with dainty bright lemon-yellow flowers. *Chicory* is brilliant
lavender-blue and pops up even in sidewalk cracks.

I'd tell you about pussytoes, Oswego tea, and selfheal, but it
would just be the blind leading the blind. I've only just begun to
know my way around the bush. Most wildflowers are just names
to me, albeit some of the most fascinating names going—creeping
Charlie, red-knees, bite-tongue, witch's moneybag, kiss-me-Dick,
beggar's-ticks, slobber weed, welcome-to-our-house, pukeweed,
frog's mouth, kiss-me-over-the-garden-gate, fussy Gussy, lady's

Daisy fleabane   Chicory   Bouncing bet

washbowl, ass's foot, widow's tears, nap-at-noon, sleepy Dick, and eleven o'clock lady (the last three are all sobriquets for star of Bethlehem).

I'm still trying to find out what the beautiful red stuff is that blankets the fields of North and South Carolina in early spring. Every native I asked had the same ready answer: "Honey, that's just a lil' ole wee-yud!" I brought it home with me anyway, some dried and some pressed, and one of these days I'll track it down. (Weed handbooks are impossible. Whether they're for fun or for real, it takes weeks to identify one wildling.)

Funny-looking weeds

Dainty flowering weeds are kid stuff to garden clubbers. It's nature's oddballs they really love, like *teasel*. I'm sure you've seen teasel at flower shows and at the florist's. It's the chubby oval burr with quills like a porcupine. Why pay for it when it runs wild in the fields? Even easier to find are *milkweed pods* (the ones you can spot at high speed on the thruway). Be sure to remove the milky-white floss from the long, winged pods before you dry them. It flies all over the place later and will take you days to clean up. *Butterfly weed* is a fancy cousin of milkweed, with bright orange flowers (check your state-protected list).

Another highway hugger is *staghorn sumac*. In the fall its brilliant red berries and deep red velvety leaves can't help but catch your eye. *Cattails* are often found in marshes and swamps (pick them early, before the "tails" are full). *Dock*, as everybody thinks everybody knows but I didn't for years, is the spiky weed with curly seed heads that grows everywhere. Most people pick it when it's dark chocolate-brown, but the earlier stages are interesting too—green, pink, beige, caramel, and copper.

Grasses, grains, and other "junk"

They say that guests know all about you the minute they walk in the door. I don't remember what dazzling arrangement I had in the front hall last year, but this year I have weeds—the ones you see in the chapter frontispiece. Given half an opening, I'll describe them to one and all. The tall, smoky plumes are marsh grass, plucked on the turnpike as the trucks whooshed by. The pale silvery grasses are from last summer's ocean vacation. The bleached-blond things with "wings" are milkweed pods found by the local bowling alley. There are also pussy willows, goldenrod, a dried sunflower head, a dried California artichoke that started its drying-out process in our son's suitcase, and—the pièce de résistance—swirly, curly corn tassels and ribbonlike leaves from my own two-by-four corn field last year. And the clouds of poor girl's baby's breath? Don't ask me. I yanked whatever-it-is out of the garden at fall clean-up.

Do you begin to get the idea? Never throw away anything. Never come home from anywhere empty-handed. The world is full of fascinating grasses, and there are also beautiful grains like wheat, oat, millet, and rye. Pick wild grasses before the Fourth of July to keep their lacy, soft green color. Spray both grains and grasses with hair spray or plastic to keep them from flying all over. And don't forget the "et ceteras." At home or abroad, look for leaves, wild berries, interesting branches, weathered wood, oddly shaped roots, lichen, fungi, gourds, bark, rocks, vines, and rushes. You never know what "find" you might stumble on.

Have you ever heard of *equisetum?* It's a rush with grooved and jointed hollow stems something like bamboo. I saw it at a flower show and assumed it was a rare, exotic, and expensive plant that I'd have to order from the florist. Not so. I can pick it less than a mile from my house, thanks to a tip from a big-hearted garden-club friend, but I can't tell you *where* under pain of death. Even weed pickers like to keep their finds to themselves.

By the sea, by the sea

I used to think that shells and driftwood were the only things to look for at the beach. Now I leave the shells and (good hunting!) driftwood to the other beachcombers and happily gather their leavings. I collect pebbles and rocks of all kinds. I collect anything with a hole in it—to string as jewelry, to hang in mobiles and wind chimes, or to use as flower containers. I collect colored glass, twigs, and things that look like other things—animals, birds, valentine hearts, people's feet, or maybe a baked potato (I'll figure out what to *do* with them later).

I look for grasses and beach flowers and take cuttings from dune plants like dusty miller. Of course I don't turn down starfish, sand dollars, coral, sea urchins, barnacles, and other dryable sea animals. But mostly I pick up things I've never noticed before, things I would have run away from screaming a few years ago, things that only a garden clubber could love. (I don't pick up jellyfish, but in my zeal I once pounced on a strange new formation that turned out to be Rover's dried you-know-what.) Here is some slimy "seaweed" that I fished out of the ocean last month. It dried beautifully and turned out to be devil's-finger sponge (7) and orange sea wand (1) (with sea animal still attached). The white curlicue is dried California kelp. Number 2 is a chunk from the white cliffs of Dover (it's coal-black inside and looks something like a penguin). Number 3 is a double-barreled shell holding dried paperwhite narcissus. Number 4 is a California kelp root, marvelously striated in black, brown, and white. (I gave a piece

1   2   3   4   5   6   7

to a friend who promptly mounted it on a walnut base and gave it a place of honor on a glass-top table.) Number 5 is another sponge from a Carolina beach, along with fuzzy beach grass. Number 6 is a chunk of crystal found on the shores of Aruba. (Another friend paid six hundred dollars in Jamaica for a giant-size edition, but don't think she has rocks in her head. She could probably sell it tomorrow for one thousand dollars.) The "containers" are holey beach rocks.

If you'd still rather stick to pretty seashells, here's what to do with them after you get them home. Wash and scrub them in warm soapy water, then rinse in clear water and bleach in a Clorox and water solution. Rinse and wash again. To make them shiny, rub with baby oil or machine oil cut with lighter fluid.

Pinecones, pods, and nuts

Wreaths made of all-natural materials are big in garden-club circles (and high-dollar in florist's shops). But here's where lazy girls and I part company briefly. I learned about pinecone wreaths from the horse's mouth—from Mrs. William A. Bridges, who learned from artisans in the Smoky Mountains of North Carolina, who learned from the French Broad River Garden Club Foundation, who borrowed the Elizabethan art from Grimling

Gibbons, who was chief wood carver for Sir Christopher Wren. In other words, I do it the hard way. If you're thinking of doing a quickie wreath with styrofoam, linoleum paste, a few dozen look-alike cones, and artificial fruit, this lesson is not for you. But if you want to break your nails, bruise your thumbs, scratch your arms, and smell up your kitchen for the sake of a Grimling Gibbons-type heirloom, here's how.

Start gathering your materials in August for a Christmas wreath. You'll need between one and two hundred separate pieces —sweet gum balls, horse chestnuts, cotton burrs, peach pits, acorns, hickory nuts, prune seeds, burdock pods, beech pods, and walnuts—plus every kind of cone you can find, from tiny hemlock to white pine. You'll soon get into the habit of looking down when you walk, instead of straight ahead. You can send away for more exotic materials, such as the deodara cedar "roses" and green piñon cones that you see here. Try Western Tree Cones, 1925 Brooklane, Corvallis, Oregon 97730. (Or a dear California friend may have an obliging cone-picking daughter.)

Next come soaking and baking. Soak the cones in water for two to three hours, then bake them on aluminum foil with a top covering of damp newspapers for five to six hours at 150 degrees. Be sure to slice some cones in half to create "flowers." Nuts and acorns are also prebaked.

Next you have to wire each piece individually with florist's wire. To make holes in nuts, seeds, and acorns, use an electric drill. Or you can wire a small square of nylon stocking around each one and then wire them into clusters. For the base of your wreath, cut pegboard into a doughnut shape with a jigsaw, and drill still more holes for the wires to go through (remember, you have hundreds of things to wire on). Plan your design and start with the largest cones first. When you get to the finishing layers, it will help to prop the wreath on an easel so that light will shine through the holes.

If you really can't resist a touch of color, wire clusters of red pistachio shells into rosettes. Or add naturally dried fruits in Della Robbia style. Spray your finished masterpiece with clear plastic to polish and preserve it. Add a backing of felt to hide the tangle of wires and to protect your walls. There's no need to put your "wood carving" away with the Christmas balls, but if you store it (in a sealed plastic bag), be sure to add a handful of mothballs to keep bugs and things away.

More nutty ideas

If you don't have the patience for a big, chunky wreath, try a pinecone crescent, swag, candle bobeche, "tree," or kissing ball. And if you honestly can't see what pinecone wreaths have to do with flower arranging, here's a real lazy-girl trick: Fasten sliced pinecone "flowers" to extra-heavy wires or sticks. Spray-paint them any color under the sun and "arrange."

You can also wire sweet gum balls into frankly fake flowers. Tulip-tree pods can be pulled apart and glued to a pinecone to look like a giant flower. If you have a huge western pinecone, glue on dried seed pods of evening primrose, plant in a clay pot, and trim with ribbon. And what's wrong with a simple basket heaped with cones and dried flowers or weeds? I've seen them in sophisticated beige and white penthouses as well as in America's historic-landmark homes.

Look up in the air, too, when you're nature walking. Many trees, such as sycamore, magnolia, catalpa, bladder nut, golden rain, and mimosa, have odd pods that are yours for the picking. And let's not forget honey-locust pods. If you're ever railroaded into a Garden Club of America flower show, here's how I won a ribbon my very first time out. Sure, it's ugly. I wouldn't have it in the house. But for a flower show, the funnier-looking the weed, the better. (For the arrangement, I removed the seeds from the pods to show off the satiny blond insides. With a rock dug out of the garden, swirls of aluminum wire, and multicolored fishing line, plus a few maranta leaves, who was to say it didn't look like a Jackson Pollock painting?) You can also spray-paint honey-locust pods in wild colors, or gild them for chic but cheap gift ties.

More "yes-yes's" than "no-no's"

I'm all for conservation. If we don't stop picking our wild plants willy-nilly, there won't be any left for our children's children. Before you go gathering, find out what's pickable and what isn't. Ask a local garden club or your state conservation chairman, or write to the National Council of State Garden Clubs, 4401 Magnolia Avenue, St. Louis, Missouri 63110.

But conservationists have raised such a ruckus that many people are afraid to pick anything outside their own backyard. In fact, I know garden clubbers who think dogwood is taboo even if it's their own. That's silly. What does a nursery-grown tree outside your window have to do with denuding the nation's forests? Just follow a few courteous, commonsense rules.

Don't pick in local, state, or federal parks, preserves, or sanctuaries. Don't pick on private property without getting the owner's permission. (I wouldn't dream of asking for a free ear of corn, but, having discovered corn tassels, I'm going to knock on the nearest farmer's door and pick corn tassels till the cows come home.) Don't be piggy and pick all the flowers on a plant—leave some for the next flower lover. Shake out the seeds from pods, cones, and capsules where they grow.

Don't dig up dune or swamp plants that don't stand a chance in your suburban garden, but don't be afraid to transplant a tiger lily, violet, or black-eyed Susan, roots and all, that will flourish just as well in captivity—and save you a lot of steps. You can keep a rooted violet "arrangement" in the house for weeks before setting it out again. Here's one two months after it was dug up to decorate a "sculpture" our daughter had carved from a cedar log rescued from the firewood bin. It bloomed cheerfully for weeks, even though you can see it's trying hard to find the sun.

Even an especially bright and chubby dandelion clump can fill in for cut flowers. Finally, don't forget that any plant on the protected list is better off in your garden than six feet under a bulldozer. Watch for areas scheduled for development—you'll do yourself and the world a favor by rescuing a doomed jack-in-the-pulpit or fringed gentian.

NOT OKAY TO PICK

California poppy
Dutchman's-breeches
hepatica
Indian pipe
lady's slipper

moccasin flower
pipsissewa
trailing arbutus
trillium

PICK ALL YOU WANT

aster
black-eyed Susan
boneset
bouncing bet
butter-and-eggs
buttercup
chicory
clover
daisy
dandelion
day lily
goldenrod
jewelweed
Joe-pye weed

milkweed
morning glory
mullein
mustard
pearly everlasting
pokeweed
Queen Anne's lace
skunk cabbage
sunflower
tansy
thistle
violet
yarrow

4

The "Branch Arrangement"

THE MORE YOU LEARN about flower arranging, the crazier you'll be about branch arrangements. You've probably been doing branch arrangements for years and didn't know it. Have you ever filled the house in spring with golden boughs of forsythia? Have you ever brought home autumn leaves or pussy willow from the corner street vendor? These are branch arrangements, to be sure. But let me ask you this—have you ever dragged home a dead branch you found lying in the gutter? You will, you will. Once you develop a garden clubber's eye for branches, you'll find treasures everywhere—along the highways and byways, in the woods and on the beach, in the piles of garden prunings your neighbors put out for the trash man, and even at the city dump.

Back in your own backyard

You might as well start with the branches right under your nose. Flowering branches are a natural, of course. Just add a con-

tainer and water and, voilà! an arrangement. Some favorite flowering trees you might have are apple, peach, pear, plum, crab apple, dogwood, magnolia, star magnolia, and redbud. Popular flowering shrubs include azalea, weigela, viburnum (snowball), Japanese quince, flowering almond, spirea (bridal wreath), mock orange, hydrangea, rhododendron, and forsythia. Others that aren't quite so well known, especially by their botanical handles, are buddleia (butterfly bush), kolkwitzia (beauty bush), potentilla (buttercup bush), deutzia, heath, and heather.

Take your time selecting branches to cut, and don't be greedy. One well-chosen, perfectly shaped branch is a better arrangement than a slap-dash vaseful. And, as I keep saying, don't forget that buds are often more beautiful than blossoms. A budded magnolia branch makes a great Easter egg tree, by the way, and yes, of course, the buds will open (if you don't forget to water).

Leaf buds are pretty, too. You don't have to wait for non-

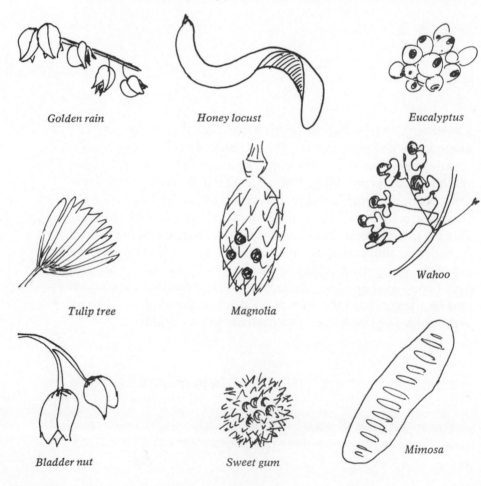

Golden rain   Honey locust   Eucalyptus

Tulip tree   Magnolia   Wahoo

Bladder nut   Sweet gum   Mimosa

flowering trees and shrubs to burst into green before picking them. You can see the line of the branch much better before it's in full foliage. "Line" is what you're after, and three graceful budded sprays of maple, witch hazel, or birch may be all you need. Pussy willow can be coaxed into fascinating swirls by bending and wiring it for a few hours (add a bit of pachysandra). Most needled evergreens have good line. Pine, cedar, hemlock, and yew are all likely candidates for branch arrangements. Add a few sprigs of juniper and privet to yew for texture contrast.

In the fall, you'll probably be more interested in color than in line. Pick boughs of blazing maple or golden oak for an instant arrangement (and preserve them in glycerin for next year. See Chapter 7). Hang a satiny, silvery beech limb against a white wall for an instant "sculpture" (spray it to make the curled and twisted leaves hang on even longer). In late fall, there are bright berried branches like pyracantha, holly, bittersweet, and the viburnums. Or jump the gun and pick some while they're still green. And don't overlook branches with interesting seed pods and fruit, such as honey locust, sweet gum, tulip tree, mimosa, magnolia, bladder nut, eucalyptus, golden rain, and wahoo.

Garden-club goodies

Unfortunately, some of the most elegant branches aren't found in everybody's yard. You'll probably have to ask a garden-club friend for aucuba, nandina or osmanthus, which I've described back in Chapter 1. Another flower arranger's pet is *cotoneaster*, which is pronounced "kah-tonny-as'ter," not "cotton-Easter." It has teensy shiny-green leaves on slender, arching branches. *Photinia* has large spiny leaves, showy white flowers, and red fruits. *Trifoliate orange* has lethal-looking spikes that only a garden clubber would tangle with. *Hickory* has velvety pale brown buds. Twisty *Corylus contorta* is called Harry Lauder's Walking Stick.

Actually, the classier the species is, the harder it is to describe, but here goes. *Fantail willow* looks like a pussy willow that's gone bananas. Irresistible. *Cedrus atlantica* (Atlas cedar) looks like

clusters of silvery-blue stars. *Euonymus alatus* looks like a Tinker Toy made out of cork. It's as different from plain euonymus as Marjorie Main was from Marilyn Monroe. It's also called "winged euonymus." *Winged sweet gum* is interesting, too.

One last curiosity is *Cornus alba*, or "bloodtwig dogwood." As I learned after I planted it, it's nothing like the dogwood you and I know. It's a dense, fast-growing shrub famous for its branches, which turn bright red in winter. It looks great in the snow and also in your living room. Toss an armful of soaring blood-twigs into a floor container and you're through arranging for the season.

To force a forsythia

It's always fun to get a jump on spring. A few boughs of creamy dogwood or rosy cherry blossoms go a long way toward chasing the midwinter blahs, and it's easy to hurry them along. Easy, but iffy. Forcing branches is anything but an exact science; every hard-and-fast rule is qualified by "except for" or "depending on." But don't let that hold you back. If it's all guesswork anyway, your guess may be as good as the experts'.

How soon can you cut branches for forcing? That depends. It depends on the normal blooming time of the tree or shrub and also its normal bud-to-bloom timetable. Generally, six weeks before blooming is the earliest you can pick. That would be some-time in February in most areas.

The one thing all experts agree on is that you must pick on a mild, balmy day, preferably after a rain. After that, there are as many recommended procedures as there are pussies on a willow, but give this one a try. Split or pound the ends of the stems, place them in deep, tepid water, and set them in a dark place for three days. I don't know why the dark-room treatment makes a differ-ence, but it does. Move the branches into the light until the buds are about to burst, then move them to a sunny window. Spray them occasionally with a plant atomizer.

Some common plants you can force are apple and crab apple, azalea, andromeda, laurel, pear, and quince. Forsythia and pussy willow are the quickest and easiest (about two weeks); dogwood takes the longest (four to five weeks).

Trees do grow in Brooklyn, etc.

City girls get short shrift when it comes to branches. Metropolitan florist shops just aren't as big as all outdoors. The only really interesting branch you'll find at most florists' is *manzanita*, the weirdly twisted California native known as "ghost wood." But of course you'll find greens (all the ones mentioned in Chapter 1). I won't go through the list again, but I will repeat, loud and clear, that nature isn't perfect or sacrosanct. Garden clubbers never, never use anything "as is." If your florist's branches are dull and uninteresting, *make* them interesting.

Peel that wisteria. Bend that forsythia. Curl that magnolia leaf. Use all of the tricks in Chapter 6 and Chapter 12—like merrily pruning away extra leaves, like giving pine a haircut, like soaking and tying Scotch broom and cutting or tearing leaves into new shapes. Branch arrangers can be even more brutal. You can prune needled evergreens to within an inch of their lives for a stiff, stark, modern effect. In fact, you can strip them of all their foliage and use just the bold, bare "bones." Even the most humdrum branch can acquire distinction if it is chopped and lopped into beautiful, blunt angles and lines. When your forsythia is on its last legs, swish the stems clean and you've got "poor girl's Scotch broom."

Does that sound as if all branch arrangements are kooky? I'll grant you that, by the nature of the beast, it's easy to end up with a tortured, arty, flower-show look. But pruning doesn't necessarily mean scalping. Be gentle with your editing if you want an old-fashioned, natural-looking arrangement. Know when to stop, like the Japanese. Or did you think all Japanese branch arrangements were stilted and naked as a peeled egg? Not so. They can be as lovely and airy as a wheat field in the wind. Here, a bough of Japanese maple looks twice as nice with half its leaves removed so that each one stands out in graceful silhouette.

Everybody take a bough

The best part about branch arranging is that, suddenly, everybody's rich. The woods, fields, and shores are a treasure trove of leafy or flowering trees and shrubs. Never pick wild dogwood or any other plant on your state's protected list, but almost any evergreen is yours for the asking. Then there are vines. Everybody makes such a fuss over wisteria that you'd think it was the only vine that grows. Wild vines can be twisted, curled, peeled, and bent into fascinating shapes, too. Dried vines with fresh flowers are very Japanesy, also 1970s chic. (Don't forget your clippers—vines are tough customers.)

Look on the ground for fallen limbs and broken twigs, especially after a storm. Look for slabs of bark and gnarled root formations. At the beach, of course, you'll look for driftwood. But these days you'll find more driftwood in the shell shops than in the dunes. Get smart and scavenge for driftwood where you're most likely to find it—in the woods. Any piece of wood that's been weathered by sun, wind, and rain is "driftwood" to me. The best place to look is along the banks of brooks and streams. Since woodsy wood is more apt to be buggy than beachy wood is, it's extra wise to treat it before you put it on display in your living room. Scrub it clean and then bleach it in one part Clorox to two parts water for a day or two. Dry it in the sun, than rub it with a piece of cotton soaked in linseed oil.

When you're out driving, look for dead or alive branches along little-used country roads as well as busy thruways. In fact, have you ever thought of getting your state's roads commission to do your cutting for you? State and local highway workmen are always out trimming and pruning and won't mind a bit if you help them pick up. One friend of mine not only sweet-talked her way into a gold mine of blazing orange pyracantha, but had it delivered to her door! The gas and electric companies and telephone companies are big pruners, too. Just follow your ears to the buzz saw.

Bare and beautiful

Lemon leaves and apple blossoms are all very well, but the ultimate in branch arranging is bare branches. Stark, naked branches as nude as a skinny-dipper. Probably the most famous bare branch is our exotic old friend manzanita, but there are exotica on the East Coast, too—almost any one of the "garden-club" branches already mentioned is twice as garden-clubby when denuded of its leaves. There are also regional oddities that might be called branches, such as the cypress "knees" of the South (they tell me they're actually cypress roots that bump out of the swamp so the tree can "breathe"). Look for these strange, sculptural knobs in dozens of roadside stands through Georgia.

My favorite unbranch is a piece of New Jersey swamp cedar (the same cedar that went into the shingles on Independence Hall). It has marvelous whorls and swirls, and considering that it was verified by Rutgers University to be ten to twenty thousand years old, I think it was a steal at $1.50. It could stand all alone as a "sculpture." Here, with dried field mullein and chunks of optical quartz, it's a "branch arrangement," no?

But don't let me scare you off. The best bare branches of all are the simple, ordinary kind that everybody has. The most beautiful bare-branch arrangement ever created is the stark winter landscape right out your window. Notice all the different patterns etched against the sky. Notice how some branches swirl and curve gracefully, while others make sharp, jagged angles. When you're so busy looking at naked trees you start climbing telephone poles, you're on your way to becoming a branch arranger.

Look at branches up close, too. Dogwood has little bumps that look like tiny turbans. Star magnolia has "pussy willows" all winter long. Crape myrtle is as smooth as gray satin. Every branch is different, but not every branch is beautiful. Shop around—the whole outdoors is your marketplace. But most of all, keep your eyes open around the house. Were you going to throw out that dead magnolia branch? Did you think your Christmas greens were shot just because their needles had dropped? Garden clubbers never throw away anything. Their basements and garages are filled with skeletons from old arrangements, ready to be whisked into bare-branch bouquets.

Gilding the limb

You can give your bare branches a whole new look with a can of spray paint. Good old flat white works wonders. I've seen puny bunches of white-sprayed twigs for $1.50 at a country stand, and more elegant ones in a posh shop at $5.00 per branch. Why not pot a whole small dead tree in plaster of Paris and give it a coat of bright white? Plant it in the living room to go with your see-through tables and beanbag chairs, or give it to your teenage daughter to hang her bangles, baubles, and beads on.

The sketch at the beginning of the chapter is the corpse of a dear departed baby boxwood that was sprayed white and "arranged" in a 99¢ plastic photo cube. Instead of dried Queen Anne's lace, it sometimes wears dried pansies or bright zinnia buttons, milkweed pod "birds," fresh greens, or one huge fresh red flower. It also sometimes sits in the same room with an enormous full-blown bouquet of amazingly gaudy dried field and garden flowers, and why not? (People's boxwoods are always dying—just ask around.)

White branches make great Christmas "trees" strung with tiny ornaments and minilights—and Easter egg "trees," too. Use a simple cluster of snow-white switches tied in the middle with a scarlet velvet bow for a door piece. Designer Edward Stiffler lacquers grapevines bright white or shiny black and swirls them into one-of-a-kind wreaths trimmed with white silk morning glories and silky pink roses.

You can literally gild your branches with gold or silver spray paint. Given a metallic coat, the dead boxwood above could pass for an expensive wire sculpture. Or why not paint your boughs hot-pink, orange, pea-green or passion-purple? Even straight, twiggy branches in crazy mixed-up colors can be as exciting as a modern abstract painting.

Out and far out on a limb

Once you've graduated from lovely pink apple-blossom sprays to purple-painted sticks, you'll start seeing "branches" everywhere. City girls can use ordinary garden stakes from the hardware store. Try breaking and bending them into different angles, the way garden clubbers do, before you arrange them. Another favorite with arrangers is the long, fat bamboo pole that rugs come rolled around. Cut into varying lengths, it's used for all

kinds of contemporary and Japanese designs (as well as for containers and bases). Some friendly rug stores hand them out gratis. Instead of vines, you can use reeds sold for basket making, or how about embroidery hoops? Wiggle your imagination and these are branches, too—curtain rods, wire, metal pipes, broomstraws, drinking straws, toothpicks, and—don't laugh—spaghetti. (Combine skinny spaghetti stems with fluted pasta sticks, wheat stalks, and strawflowers in a pewter tankard for a long-lasting kitchen arrangement or quickie pizza party decoration.)

5
Frankly Fake

Is IT EVER OKAY to use artificial flowers? No and yes. No, with a capital yech, if you mean "just like real" flowers made of plastic. Yes, if you mean flowers made of anything—but anything—but plastic. Even drugstore cotton balls stuck on a bare branch are better than the most expensive custom-made plastic arrangement you can buy (Seriously. Wire them on with a little brown tissue paper and brown florist's tape.)

I know, I know—it takes willpower to resist plastic flowers. They're sold in every store in town, from snootiest boutique to five-and-dime. Some of your best—and richest—friends use plastic flowers. And, after all, who can tell the difference? Why, some plastic flowers look so real you have to stick your nose in them to tell they're not. True. That's why they're so awful. If you're going to cheat, you have to cheat big. Stick to fake flowers that are frankly phony, unabashedly ersatz, and barefacedly bogus. Who needs plastic when you can buy (or make) fabulous frauds made of paper, wood, metal, fabric, sisal and straw, cardboard, seashells, wire, glass, beads, enamel, or porcelain?

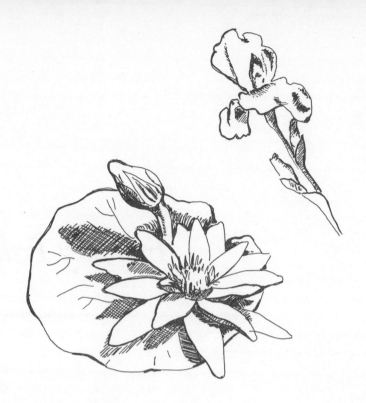

Forever-and-ever fakes

Don't think all frankly fake flowers are cheap. You can get a charming Burgues porcelain water lily for $175. Or a simple daffodil thing for $450. Gorham has a whole "forever garden" of bouquets hand-enameled over 24-karat gold plate that range from $600 to a mere $70. Even plebeian bone china flowers are out of a poor girl's class at $5 to $35. But, just in case you're a rich little poor girl who's been ruining her *House Beautiful* decor with tenement-style tulips, you might consider the investment. A floral work of art will last forever, just like your Aubussons and Dufys. If you're the artistic type, you don't have to settle for a ready-made arrangement—you can buy single stems to fix yourself. An exquisite Boehm porcelain blue iris goes for $175. A smaller yellow rose is only $100. Oh, well—after browsing through porcelain flowers, you'll scarcely turn a hair at the prices of glass and bead flowers.

Silk flowers are next on a poor girl's forget-it list. You can pay up to $35 for a single bloom; $350 for a buxom bouquet. How about metal flower "sculptures"? They were absurdly high priced when they first came out, but, like all good ideas, they've been copied to death. Do look for handmade brass, copper, and other metal flowers at craft shows. You may come home with a beautiful bargain from a struggling young artisan.

Flower, flower on the wall

Another kind of fake flower is a flower painting, and I don't mean still another reproduction of Van Gogh's *Sunflowers*. Artists have always been fascinated by flowers, from Ming Dynasty painters on porcelain up to pop artist Andy Warhol. If you must settle for a reproduction, make it a "now" one. Look for Georgia O'Keefe's luminous *Yellow Calla Lily*, Ellsworth Kelly's stark lithograph *Cyclamen 111*, Alex Katz's pale purple irises against a fiery red background, or one of Lowell Nesbitt's huge flowery canvases (he doesn't paint anything *but* flowers). Better still, look for originals at poor-girl prices. Keep your eye out at art-school exhibitions, outdoor art shows, and even the annual "art night" at your local high school. Teenagers are loaded with talent—and they are not very good at bargaining. I paid $8 for a wildly imaginative flower painting that must have cost the young man $8 in thick, drippy oil paint alone. (It's so wild that even he couldn't decide which end was up, so he signed it both top and bottom. Terrific.)

Or be your own artist. Make a bright, splashy collage of flowers cut from seed catalogs and magazines. Cover a folding screen with *New Yorker* covers (their artists are some of the best in the business, and they're always painting flowers). Twist easy-to-bend aluminum or copper wire into flower shapes (daffodils turn out great), or copy the metal centerpiece that dotted the tables at a gala Garden Club of America annual banquet. It's nothing but brass spirals and fresh leatherleaf fern in a brass cartridge.

Phony as a three-dollar bluebell

But let's get down to ordinary, affordable fakes — the kind of fake flowers that most people mean by fake flowers. New and clever make-believe flowers spring up as fast as the artsy-craftsy boutiques that sell them. Look for giddy, gaudy fabric flowers made of burlap, felt, denim, calico prints, and cotton eyelet. Look for big, bold blossoms jigsawed out of wood, and perky little posies cut out of cardboard. Look for airy wire flowers, delicate shell flowers, chubby straw and sisal flowers, and glossy papier-mâché flowers. Now that everybody's getting into the handicraft art, there's no telling what bright new idea some bright young thing will come up with next.

You may even spot unexpected treasures in department stores along with the tacky plastics. I've found "poor girl's" silk roses made of synthetics, charming china carnations, assorted glass and molded-plastic flowers in unreal shapes and colors, and some fascinating half-real half-fake Mexican imports in muted beige tones. All of these ranged between $1.25 and $2.75 per flower, with cheap-looking fabric poppies the highest and the Mexican stunners the lowest. Come to think of it, that's about what you pay for better plastic flowers, which doesn't justify the price of either. All store-bought fake flowers are overpriced, if you ask me. Just try to remember that they last longer than fresh ones at the same price.

God bless Dennison's

Haven't I forgotten something? What about paper flowers? Paper flowers are the most fabulous fakes of all. I've never met a paper flower I didn't like, from exotic boutique beauty to a kindergartner's first try. If you can't afford fresh flowers, can't be bothered with dried flowers, and can't find any acceptable weeds, stick with paper and you can't go wrong.

Paper flowers are one thing you won't find in department stores and five-and-dimes, thanks be. You still have to hunt for them. Try the shops in town that specialize in the unusual—you know, the ones with names like Et Cetera, Calico Cat, and Flowers and Fancies. Import shops are another good bet—the Orientals are old hands with paper. Best of all, track down a wholesaler who sells window-display goodies to department stores.

Never buy what you can make

Paper flowers may be cheap compared to Boehm porcelains, but $2.50 for one crepe-paper peony is ridiculous. Unless you have two left hands and ten thumbs, make your own. You'll find patterns for paper flowers everywhere—in library books, how-to pamphlets, women's magazines, and maybe along with your crepe paper. They can be as cinchy or as complicated as you like. All you need are tissue or crepe paper, florist's wire, florist's tape, glue, and, if you want to be fancy, almost any old thing for centers— beads, buttons, gift-wrap yarn pompons, ball fringe, pods, cones, or store-bought stamens. You can get by with inexpensive dime-store paper for most flowers, but do get the "good stuff" for your leaves. Dime-store green is ghastly.

What's your favorite flower? There are knock-out patterns for poppies, peonies, zinnias, mums, carnations, asters, and of course roses. You can whip up country-fresh daisies and sunflowers, springlike tulips, daffodils, and irises, or the most exotic lilies, anemones, and hibiscus. Best of all, you can create way-out flowers that never grew in anybody's garden. Most paper-flower patterns are larger than life-size, and the bigger and bolder you build them, the better. I've made black-eyed Susans a yard wide. (Bend wire coat hangers into petal shapes, wrap with yellow crepe paper, and poke into a black-painted styrofoam round. Back with a green crepe-paper "calyx" and mount on a dahlia stake or old broom handle.) But the newest-looking boutique bouquet I've seen was a basket of *smaller* than life-size mixed flowers. To copy it, just scale down your patterns, and don't be a stickler for realism. How about turquoise zinnias, hot-pink daffodils, yellow anemones, and a few orange you-name-its?

A shaggy mum story

Suppose you see a new and different boutique flower that you know won't be in any book? Buy just one. Take it home, tear it apart to see how it's done, and turn out a whole dozen for the price of one. I fell in love with the shaggy white mums at the beginning of the chapter years ago and naively blew $12 on them. It seemed a shrewd investment at the time. Needless to say, when the original batch finally succumbed to dust, humidity, and fireplace smoke, I replaced them with a dollar's worth of crepe paper.

To make a shaggy mum, cut a standard 20″ x 10′ package of white crepe paper into thirds (about 6½″ wide). Make 4″ cuts about ½″ apart along one edge, cutting through the entire thickness of the pack. Use sharp pinking shears if you have them. For the center, make similar 2½″ cuts in a 5″ x 18″ fold of yellow crepe paper; unroll and reroll tightly. Unroll the fringed white paper and wrap it tightly around the yellow center, being careful to keep the bottom edges aligned. For the stem, use heavy 14–18-gauge wire and wind it securely around the base of the flower. For the calyx, cut jagged points in a 4″ x 12″ strip of green crepe paper; wrap and glue it around the wired base. Cut out leaf shapes and glue two together, with a 20-gauge wire rib in between. Fasten the leaves with florist's tape as you tape the stem. Fluff out the petals. (One package of paper makes three flowers.)

Who stole the sports page?

Crepe and tissue paper aren't the only kinds of paper you can use. You can make fluffy carnations out of Kleenex (remember your senior prom?). You can make stark modern flowers out of bright cardboard rounds. You can even turn crinkled cupcake papers or foil candy papers into jiffy flowers. The newest wrinkle is egg-carton flowers. A single "cup" makes a perfect tulip, or cut out four at a time. Add wire stems, artificial stamens, ball-fringe centers, or any other zany idea you have. "Pearlized" cartons in pastel pink, yellow, or blue are made to order for lazy girls, but wouldn't ordinary cartons spray-painted black, brown, and white be more suave and sophisticated? Craft books snap, crackle, and pop with ideas, and their authors are much better at "how-to's" than I, but here's an idea you may not find in the library. The flowers are made of newspaper, yet.

To make newspaper flowers, cut five layers of newspaper into

circles and "fringe," being careful not to cut into the center. Poke
a 22-gauge wire stem through the paper center into a red ball-
fringe pompon (add a drop of glue for extra measure). To make
the leaves, cut double-thickness rectangles of red and white
polka-dot cotton. Place a rectangle of Stitch-Witchery bonding
mesh in between; add a length of 22-gauge wire in the center, and
iron all together. Cut it into a leaf shape and attach it to the stem
with florist's tape. Plant in a styrofoam-filled clay pot.

Frankly fabric-ated

Thanks to Stitch-Witchery, every last fabric there is can be
turned into a beautiful bloom. Stitch-Witchery is a magic two-

sided iron-on bonding mesh that you'll find in the sewing department of most stores. Sandwiched between two layers of cloth, it adds all the body you need. Cut out daisies, anemones, fringed circles, or your own fanciful shapes (it's easier to cut out your flowers after the fabrics are bonded).

You can also use many paper-flower patterns just as well on fabric. Try making mums, poppies, or carnations out of whatever sewing scraps you have on hand. If your tulips are black and white striped and your cornflowers are red plaid taffeta, so much the better. But don't attempt fancy silk roses or organdy camellias without a specific fabric-flower pattern. Silk's a little trickier than crepe paper. Stiffened burlap ribbon is easy to work with. It's sold by the yard in florist's shops and can be cut into all sorts of jaunty flower shapes. Add stamen centers. Or gather ordinary cotton eyelet edging into airy, daisylike flowers, with beads, buttons, or pompons for centers. Then there's felt—good old felt. On page 71 you'll see one of the jiffiest, spiffiest felt-flower arrangements you could put on your table at a ladies' luncheon or New Year's Eve party.

To make a felt-flower bouquet, cut red, orange, pink, yellow, purple, and turquoise felt into four-leaf-clover shapes. Set a styrofoam ball in a champagne glass and stick flowers on with glasshead pins inserted through the center. Use just one jumbo bouquet or a grouping of several in assorted sizes. For Christmas, use red and green felt; for Easter, yellow and purple; for your daughter's birthday party, whatever her favorite colors are. Add a base of fresh green foliage if you like.

How cheap can you get?

You don't have to spend a nickel to make some of my favorite frauds. Ordinary tin-can lids can be cut, pierced, and bent into chic, expensive-looking metal flowers (use wire cutters and pliers). I've even seen flowers made out of beer-can rings. Strips of old newspaper and wheat paste are all you need for dramatic papier-mâché posies. (Or you can splurge on an extra-easy instant mix sold in hobby shops. Make some fruits and vegetables while you're at it.) Giant wooden flowers are a great idea if you're married to a handy Andy. Draw up a pattern for him and finish off your cut-out with a coat of bright paint, artistic hand decorations, or glued-on fabric.

If you're a country girl, red-painted milkweed pods make perfect poinsettias. Pinecones can be sliced into "flowers" and either left natural or enameled in gay colors. Deodara cedar "roses" and green piñon cones from the West Coast are even more flowery. If you're a city girl, be sure you buy your corn on the cob with the husks still on. Corn husks make eye-popping oversized blossoms. Just double over a dozen or so husks, staple them in the middle, and add a gilded pinecone for a center. You can also cut the husks into fat or narrow "petals" and wire them together for amazingly real looking nasturtiums, day lilies, roses, or mums. When dry, they'll stiffen into "permanent flowers."

Have you ever seen a seashell flower? Nineteenth-century New England whaling wives used to while away the lonely hours making them. Another version has it that the whalers whiled away *their* lonely hours making them and called them "sailors' valentines." In any case, it must have taken years of work, tons of patience, and thousands of teeny-tiny shells to turn out the exquisite floral wreaths. If you're a modern-day golf widow, you might want to try one. If not, how about simply drilling a hole in an ordinary oyster shell and wiring it onto a stem?

Here's one last idea I stumbled on by accident. While fooling around with Christmas candles, I discovered that soft wax can be coaxed into any shape you like. The next thing I knew, I had a whole arrangement of "roses"—for 25¢ worth of household paraffin from the supermarket and a 5¢ dish from a thrift shop. Rather than pass on my by-guess-and-by-golly method, I refer you to the how-to books in candle-making shops.

Real-live fakes

Next to blatantly bogus paper flowers, I like real-live fakes best—i.e., "rosettes" made out of fresh green leaves. Some of these are also mentioned in other chapters, but I'll lump them all together here to show you what wondrous "flowers" you have right at hand or can buy for pennies at the florist's. I call gera-

Ivy

Geranium

Sedum

Palm

Hosta

Ginkgo

nium leaves the "poor girl's peony," sedum the "poor girl's chrysanthemum," ginkgo the "poor girl's carnation," and hosta the "poor girl's gladiolus." But you can't beat plain old ivy leaves. Actually, you can make rosettes out of almost any fresh leaf (a good way to use all those flower leaves that must be removed below the water line if you want your bouquet to last), but these are some of the fanciest. Other good bets are galax, beech, eucalyptus and pachysandra.

To make professional-looking flowers, start with a tightly wound center and add ten to twenty new "petals" in layers, wiring as you go. Finish off with a wrapping of floral tape. You can also sew through the leaves with heavy thread, or use a stapler. To make a hosta leaf gladiolus, double over four or five leaves for each blossom, using a small curly leaf for the center, and staple them together. Attach blossoms separately to stem (a hosta stalk is as good as anything). Variegated hosta makes the showiest flower. (Even out of water and stuck full of staples, hosta leaves hold up for days; and, oddly enough, they last longer without the usual presoaking.)

But you don't have to be so persnickety—you can simply cluster a bunch of leaves in your hand and wind wire around the stems. That's how the ivy "blossom" was made, with only five leaves (use smaller, paler leaves in the center). The palm was merely clipped.

P.S. on plastic

Despite my cranky caveats, *don't* throw all your plastic flowers in the garbage. They're good for something, after all. They're good for so-called Flemish flowers, if you're not sick of them yet. They're perfect for gaudy, obviously gilded Christmas decorations. Even the cheapest dime-store rose takes gold or silver paint beautifully. Bargain-basement plastic fruits can be antiqued by wiping with medium-brown stain and spraying with clear plastic. And if your plastic fakes are very, very real and you're very, very clever, you might try this trick—mix them in with the real thing. Tuck a few well-chosen leafy fakes into a collection of live houseplants to add to the jungle look. Three dewy, just-like-real roses might even pass in a bevy of fresh-cut greenery, and a few fake geraniums can perk up a nonblooming geranium plant during the winter. But even when you're mixing fake with real, the best fake is still paper. How about frankly tongue-in-cheek scarlet paper poppies pinned to your pet aspidistra some giddy party night?

6

Make the Most of Your Houseplants

———————————

BY NOW, EVERYBODY KNOWS that plants are "just like people" and have a "secret life." More people are loving, talking to, and playing pretty music for houseplants than ever before. America's living rooms have turned into jungles and its plant sellers into millionaires. (*Esquire* magazine suggests that people are raising plants instead of children because it's cheaper and safer—"Plant a child, get a lemon . . . but plant a flowering stink cactus, you get a flowering stink cactus.")

So I don't have to tell you that greenery is the most fashionable decorating accessory there is, next to art. But have you ever thought of flower arranging with your houseplants? Don't let them just sit there. The next time you talk to the spoiled-rotten darlings, ask not what you can do for them but what they can do for you.

Flower power by the pot

The simplest way to arrange with plants is to use the whole blooming pot. Actually, any grouping of potted plants might be called an arrangement. A deep bay window heaped with lush gloxinia, cineraria, and begonia is more than mere decoration, especially if it is night-lighted for extra glamor. So is an unexpected indoor garden of flowering plants on the floor of your apartment front hall. (These are a few of Dorothy Rodgers's "favorite things," in her marvelous book, *My Favorite Things*.) But massing your greenery in one spot is just the beginning of how to use houseplants in place of hothouse flowers. Why not whip up an instant centerpiece with a gift plant that's lolling around the living room? At Christmastime, drop a brilliant cherry-red cyclamen into your best silver bowl. Hide the pot of an ethereal white poinsettia with evergreen boughs and holly, and trim with Christmas balls. If all you have is a phony-looking red poinsettia, you might as well go all the way—plant red and green plaid bows on florist's wire stems right in the dirt.

At Thanksgiving, use your mum plants; on Mother's Day, geraniums. Ah, geraniums. One gaudy plant in full flower is all you need. Three or four massed together on your dinner-party table will outshine the most elegant bouquet of florist's flowers. And there's more than one kind of geranium, you know. There are dwarf types with flowers that look like carnations and miniature rosebuds and cactus flowers. There are trailing ivy geraniums with dainty all-green or green and white leaves. There's "Skies of Italy," with tricolored leaves. And don't forget the scented-leaf geraniums that smell deliciously of mint, apple, rose, or even nutmeg.

Lock, stock, and begonia

Begonia is another oldie but goodie. It comes in even more varieties than geraniums (literally hundreds). But never mind whether yours is fibrous, tuberous, or rhizomatous—if it's in flower, put it to work. And ask your favorite florist for the incredible new "Rieger" hybrid that blazes with huge colorful blooms all year round. Other flowering plants to arrange with are gardenia, camellia, fuchsia, freesia, kalanchoe, Christmas cactus, and of course all the gay spring bulbs in pots.

If you're an African violet nut, forget for a moment that they're African and treat them like plain old violets. Try planting a "bunch," soil and all, in a sparkling brandy snifter, or make them the focal point of an all-green arrangement. (A plastic bag around the root ball will keep the water mud-free.)

Speaking of mud, why not "arrange" a balled-and-bagged azalea that's on its way to your garden? If it's not too big and your table's not too small, your arranging problems are solved for weeks. One of my favorite Easter table decorations was three market baskets of pansies in a giant white soup tureen. The arrangement took two seconds and cost next to nothing, and the pansies later bloomed their heads off in the garden till Thanksgiving.

Don't forget bright berried and fruited plants, like Jerusalem cherry, ornamental Christmas peppers, and baby orange and lemon trees. Other decorative choices are natal plum "Fancy," with starry white flowers and red fruit, and kumquat "Nagami," with fragrant flowers and bright orange fruit. Both Arabian coffee and pyracantha "Red Elf" have shiny scarlet berries. Bearss dwarf lime has showy green fruit, and mistletoe fig covers itself with tiny figs.

Small-fry arrangements

Don't think you need a $50 pot of gardenias. Whisk your baby begonias off the kitchen windowsill, cluster them in a silver vegetable dish, and move them into the living room. In fact, group any of your small plants in any kind of flower container and you'll have an arrangement. Even plain green plants can be interesting if you're clever. Gather up as many different sizes, shapes, colors, and textures as you can and compose a "living landscape" for a

centerpiece. If all your plants are the same size, break up the monotony by setting some on platforms. You can use clear plastic cubes, scraps of wood, ordinary building bricks, or even children's painted blocks. Or set them on a pile-up of pretty stones for a miniature rock-garden. The idea is to vary your textures. For instance, use glass bricks with clay pots and lucite pots with clay bricks (or simply repot your plants for the evening in throwaway plastic glasses or even your best crystal). Of course, if you have elegant imported *cache pots*, you've got it made.

You don't even have to get that fancy—just line up your plants in a row. One of the most talented arrangers I know (perfectly capable of the most elaborate Victorian line-mass or classic Japanese "throw-in") set her buffet table with a smashing India print bedspread and lined up three lush ivy plants in Mexican terracotta pots. Charming. Another bright hostess decorated a blue and white luncheon table with nothing more than "Fluffy Ruffles" ferns in blue hobnail tumblers, two by two.

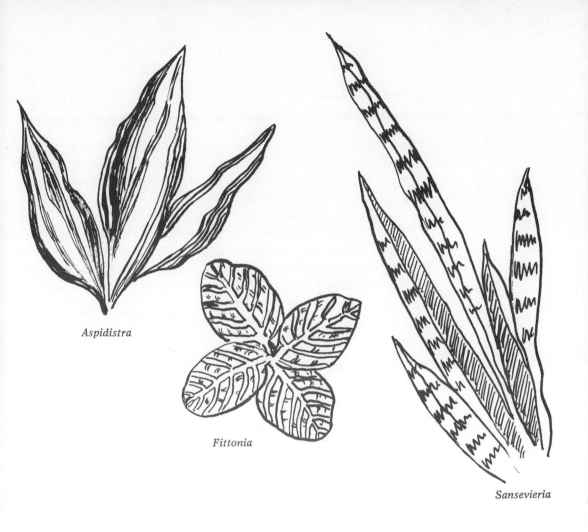

Aspidistra

Fittonia

Sansevieria

Foliage for free

It's smart to use houseplants in place of cut flowers, but that's not the half of it. The real reason garden clubbers keep plants around the house is so they can steal the leaves. Who needs fancy florist's foliage? Who needs a yard full of specimen shrubs? Almost any houseplant can supply you with all the exotic greens you need. Some arrangers keep a few favorites on a back window-sill *just* for that purpose—sort of an indoor cutting garden.

Look closely at the greens in bouquets in flower-arranging books—you'll see everything from common-as-dirt philodendron to rare and wonderful palms. Probably the most widely used leaf in arrangements is none other than good old aspidistra. The Japanese adore aspidistra. A real Ikebana pro could turn out thousands of arrangements, all different, with nothing but aspidistra leaves. Other old garden-club standbys are dieffenbachia, rubber plant, ferns, schefflera, pandanus, oxalis, castor-oil plant, and split-leaf philodendron (which is not one of the hundreds of philodendrons at all, but *Monstera deliciosa*).

You'll scarcely miss a few leaves from a big plant, but if you still have cold feet, remember that many leaves will root while they're sitting there looking pretty, and you'll soon have a whole new plant. Some plants, like wandering Jew and Chinese evergreen, grow just as happily in water—good news for flower arrangers as well as brown-thumbs.

Fancy-type foliage

So-called variegated leaves are practically an arrangement in themselves. Some green and white favorites are peperomia, fittonia, chlorophytum, dracaena, sansevieria, ivy, and pothos (the one that looks like a white philodendron).

In the begonia family alone, you'll find enough variety for a whole mixed bouquet. "Beefsteak" is known for its large round leaves that are the color of juicy rare sirloin on the underside. "Merry Christmas" has dazzling red and green markings. "Angelwing" has graceful pointed leaves with white or pink freckles. Another up-and-coming charmer, not in the begonia clan, is actually called "Freckle Face" or polka-dot plant. It may be hard to find, but ask for *Hypoestes sanguinolenta*.

Most dramatic of all are the Three C's—croton, coleus, and caladium. They're the ones that are splotched with vivid shades of crimson, pink, salmon, yellow, and white. Look what you can do with just five caladium leaves.

Maranta is in a class by itself with black polka dots on the leaves. So is *gynura*, with its velvety purple leaves. Then there is the big wide world of succulents. It would take pages to cover all the fascinating cactus-type plants that were put on earth for girls who forget to water. By all means, get to know the succulents, and start with the arranger's pet, *echeveria*. Echeveria rosettes are just as pretty as florist's roses, and they not only survive without water but sometimes root in thin air.

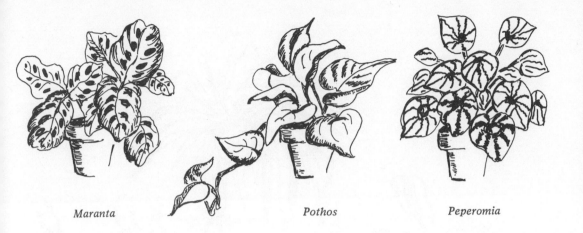

Maranta   Pothos   Peperomia

WHICH IS WHICH?

Even seasoned green-thumbs get their dieffenbachias and dra-
caenas, peperomias and fittonias mixed up. Here is a jiffy list of
the common and fancy names of old favorites that confuse most
of the people most of the time:

ASPIDISTRA—cast-iron plant (it's almost impossible to kill)

BEAUCARNEA RECURVATA—ponytail plant or bottle-palm (it has
long, twisting, curling leaves and a fat bottle-shaped trunk)

CHLOROPHYTUM—spider plant, walking iris, or airplane plant (it
spins off spiderlike babies on long airborne stems)

COLEUS—painted nettle (it's splashed with color)

CRASSULA—jade plant (the leaves are arranged in glossy green
crosses on the stem)

DIEFFENBACHIA—dumb cane or mother-in-law's tongue (the stem
has a poison that swells your tongue and leaves you speechless)

EUPHORBIA—hatrack plant (it has thick, angled, cactuslike
branches)

HOYA—wax plant (the flowers and leaves have a waxy look)

MARANTA—prayer plant (the leaves fold up at night)

MONSTERA—Swiss cheese plant or Mexican breadfruit (it has
"holes")

PANDANUS—screw pine (the leaves grow spirally in corkscrew
fashion)

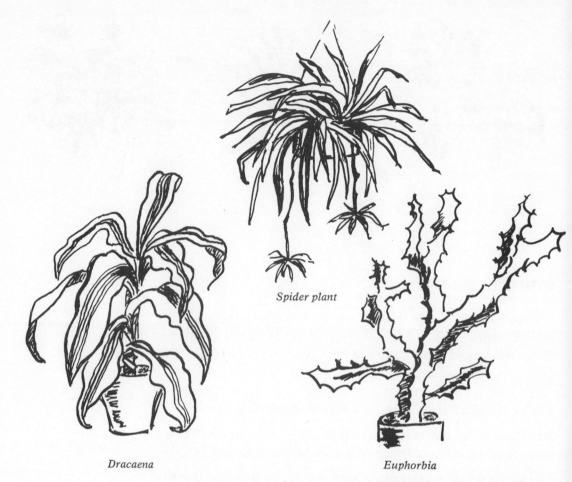

Spider plant

Dracaena

Euphorbia

Sansevieria—snake plant (the swordlike leaves look like snake-skin); also often, for some reason, called mother-in-law's tongue

Schefflera—umbrella plant (it spreads out like one)

Tradescantia or Zebrina—wandering Jew (it trails all over the place)

Do-it-yourself houseplants

Are all these fancy botanical names too much for you? Don't go away. You can also filch leaves from a sweet-potato plant, pineapple, or avocado plant—the kind you learned to grow in kindergarten. In case you had measles that week, stick a sweet potato, fat end up, in a narrow jar so that one inch is in water and half the tuber is above the neck of the jar. Keep in the dark until growth starts; then move to a bright window.

To propagate a pineapple, slice off the leafy rosette, leaving a little fruit, and dry for twenty-four hours. Dust with Rootone and plant in just enough soil to hold it steady. Moisten slightly and keep in the dark until roots form; then move to a sunny window.

To start an avocado plant, cut about a quarter inch off the top (pointed end) of the seed and suspend it (broad end down) a little way into a water-filled jar by driving three toothpicks into the sides. Place it in a warm spot and add water as needed. When the seed cracks, a seedling will appear. When it is several inches high, plant it in dirt in a small clay pot. Be patient; sometimes it takes six weeks or longer for the seed to sprout.

If you're not the patient type, plant watercress seeds that will flourish in just ten days. They'll grow in vermiculite or even in wet Kleenex. Mung-bean sprouts are even speedier. Plant them in water in a see-through container and watch them sprout in forty-eight hours.

Never leave well enough alone

If you still think houseplant leaves are a bore, there are dozens of ways you can zap them up. Garden clubbers call it "contorting," and it's much more fun than picking roses. Don't be a sissy —get out your scissors, clippers, stapler, and wire. And don't worry—the mother plant will never know how you've twisted, shaved, and scalped her offspring.

To begin with, there's "furling" and "curling." You can simply bend (or furl) a leaf into a more graceful curve. Or you can loop it over and staple it in place. For a longer-lasting curl, twist the leaf around your finger, a pencil, or a long stick for a few seconds. For a "permanent wave," wire it in place and then soak in water. If you have a huge palm leaf, wire or tape it to a bent coat hanger before soaking. You can set leaves into "pincurls" by using a stapler instead of bobby pins. You can even braid them (fun for daffodil growers who aren't supposed to plait their leaves anymore because it's bad for the bulbs).

"Rippling" is a neat trick. Do this only if no one will see the back of the leaf. Simply tape a piece of wire or a pipe cleaner down

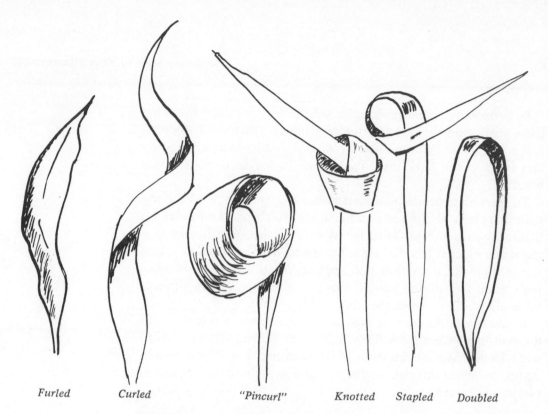

Furled   Curled   "Pincurl"   Knotted Stapled Doubled

the back rib—you'll be amazed at the acrobatic paces you can then put it through.

How about trying the "ribbon" treatment? You can simply tie a knot in broad, straplike leaves like aspidistra (also iris or yucca from the garden, and ti leaves). You can loop and staple them just like lick-and-seal gift-tie ribbon. Or you can make an extra fancy bow-knot that's just as good a focal point as any flower. Instead of a stapler, you can use straight pins, glue, or floral clay to hold your bows in place.

There are dozens of scissor tricks. Some arrangers simply tear their leaves, but you can also cut them into any size or shape you want. You can chop a leaf in half, or lop off just the top. Give pine and palm a haircut—anything from a gentle trim to a complete "butch." "Shredding" is even more fascinating. With just your thumbnail, sliver the entire inside of a leaf until it looks like a baking whisk or maybe a paper lantern (it's very Japanesy). Magnolia and avocado leaves can be "skeletonized," and castor-oil plant can be pseudo-skeletonized by pruning out the leafy flesh between the ribs.

Remember the green leaf rosettes in Chapter 5? For an even more flowery rosette, wire or staple a handful of deep red "Beef-steak" begonia leaves together. A cluster of deep brown dried rub-berplant leaves is another idea. See Chapter 7 for more about

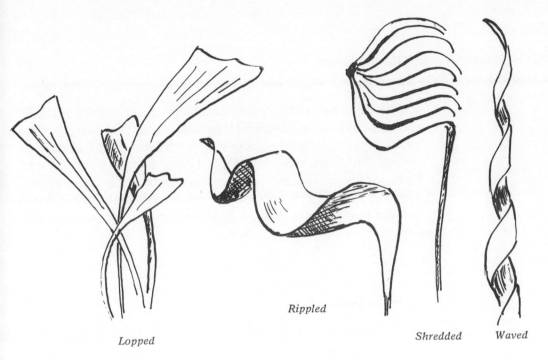

Rippled

Lopped

Shredded *Waved*

drying houseplant leaves. Or try bleaching them, Oriental-style. Immerse thoroughly dry leaves in 1 cup Clorox to 2½ to 3 gallons of water until all the color has come out (usually ten days). Rinse well in cold water and hang in the sun.

Stretching your sansevieria

You'll learn all about stretching flowers in Chapter 8, but you can stretch houseplants, too. Chances are, your own pet leaves will inspire you even more than florist's foliage. You have all year to study their curves, colorings, and quirks and to match them up with treasures from your attic, curio shelf, or vegetable bin. How about a pink-tinged echeveria rosette in a pink-tinged conch shell? How about cream-striped peperomia leaves tucked into a basket of lemons—or a bouquet of salmony croton leaves in a copper sugar bowl?

Perch a plastic-bagged African violet on a piece of weathered wood, or surround a silvery pothos with chunks of quartz. Add a few variegated geranium leaves at the base of a forced bough of dogwood.

Use your plants to stretch florist's flowers, too. Even one big golden-bronze mum will make a splash against blades of sansevieria; think what you could do with three creamy camellias and borrowings from a dieffenbachia. For an extra-quick arrangement, stick fresh flowers right into your plants (the fancy name is *pot-et-fleurs*). Liven up a trailing ivy with a few yellow daisies, or poke a bird-of-paradise into the soil of a spindly rubber plant. Even a planter spilling over with hot-pink impatiens on your summer patio will have twice as much pow with half a dozen flaming tiger lilies tucked in. It will keep your guests guessing, too.

April in December

To me, the most spectacular Christmas decoration of all is a pot of spring-fresh daffodils in bloom. But why spend $15.00 at the florist's when you can force your own for $2.50? Forcing bulbs is ridiculously easy. The hardest part is remembering to buy them 'way before Thanksgiving if you want them to bloom by Christmas.

To force paperwhite narcissus (the easiest kind and the ones you'll see pictured at the beginning of this chapter), buy at least six bulbs from any florist, garden-supply store, or even some hardware stores. Plant the bulbs pointy end up in a bowl of pebbles or gravel, covering them three-fourths of the way. Add water just to the base of the bulbs. Store them in a cool, dark place for about three weeks until well rooted and the shoots are about three inches tall. The shoots will look sickly pale, but don't worry —they'll turn green fast. Move the pot to a warmer, darkish place for a few days and then to a bright sunny window, where they'll burst into beautiful, fragrant bloom. (The whole process takes six to eight weeks.)

Once you've been wildly successful with paperwhites, you'll probably want to try your hand at more difficult daffodils, tulips, crocuses, and hyacinths. But fair warning: all of these take forever (up to three months). But here's a tip for apartment dwellers: you can store your bulbs for the first two months right in the refrigerator. You can buy special clear glass vases for hyacinths and crocuses that make the growing operation more decorative and interesting. Of course, you can also buy kits—at outrageous prices, considering the price of crocus bulbs (fifty for $3.95). A kit with six crocus bulbs and six crocus glasses costs $9.75. Twelve crocus bulbs plus a Delft bowl will set you back $7.25. A Delft bowl with four paperwhites is $8.50. Wouldn't you rather improvise with your own containers?

Unfortunately, bulbs that have been forced aren't good for much in the garden later, so you might as well toss them out. But before you scuttle that dead paperwhite, pick off some of the naturally dried silver-beige stems and blossoms. They're elegant.

7
Dried Flowers Rediscovered

ANSWER TRUE OR FALSE: (1) dried flowers are duller than yester-day's mashed potatoes; (2) dried flowers come in two colors—dishwater blond and tired-blood beige; (3) dried flowers are strictly from Colonial Williamsburg and irrelevant to glass-and-redwood girls; (4) dried flowers are the same as artificial flowers, only they get dustier.

If you answered amen to any of the above, you're as simple and naive as I was a few years back. Never in my wildest technicolored dreams did I envision dried daffodils as sunny yellow as a spark-ling April morn, dried daisies as bright-eyed as a new babe, and dried roses so fresh and pink-cheeked you could almost smell the dew. Frankly, I didn't know that daffodils and roses were dryable, period.

But modern methods have turned the old art of flower drying into a whole new ballgame, so don't yawn and run off to the next chapter. Once you discover how to keep your favorite flowers in bloom all year, and how laughably easy the whole business is, you'll never be flowerless again. And, just for the record, don't even mention once-alive dried flowers in the same breath with born-dead plastic phonies.

"But I've never dried a flower in my life"

Next to abject poverty, the best reason for taking up flower drying is devout cowardice. You can't lose. Never mind if a few old maids are bent on shrouding the art in mystique—a two-year-old can do it. You don't have to start at the bottom, live and learn, or try, try again; all you have to do is do it. Unless you're hell-bent on breaking the rules, like gathering your flowers in the rain or tumble-drying them in your automatic dryer, I promise you that you'll come up roses the very first time.

Needless to say, you won't learn all about flower drying from me. Whole books have been written on the subject. If you want to get into skeletonizing leaves, deseeding seedpods, and making pressed-flower pictures and potpourris, you can do that *later*. For now let's simply talk about how to dry a simple flower. Basically, there are three ways to dry ordinary garden flowers—in sand, in silica gel, and in thin air. Air drying is the ABC-easiest, but it only works for a handful of favorites. Silica gel is hands-down best, but it's expensive. So I'll start with sand—the oldest, cheapest, tried-and-truest way to dry almost every flower that grows.

Sand is grand

Sand drying is more fun than going back to kindergarten. If you're a career girl with a high-pressure cerebral-type job, here's your chance to get back to Mother Earth. If you're a housewife up to your ears in dirty laundry and screaming kids, now it's *your* turn to play in the sandbox. The directions go like this: get a box, put sand in the box, put your flowers in the sand, cover the flowers with sand, put the box away, and forget about it. You don't even have to cover the box. As I said, a two-year-old can do it and come up with something resembling dried flowers. Since you're not a two-year-old, you might note these finer points.

What kind of sand?

Some experts swear by builder's sand, others by children's play sand, and still others by beach sand. In other words, use whatever sand you can lay your hands on. If it's beach sand, be sure to wash it free of salt, not to mention candy wrappers, peach pits, and beer-can rings. Some experts also recommend that you sift builder's sand. The main thing is that your sand must be dryer than dry. If you like, you can concoct your own private formula by adding cornmeal, borax (break up the lumps or you'll have spotty flowers), or even kitty litter to the sand.

Put your sand in a large, sturdy box from the supermarket. Sand is *heavy*, and the books that tell you to use dress boxes were born before today's flimsy collapsibles. Shallow boxes are easier to work in and will also fit under the bed while your flowers are drying. Shoe boxes are good for beginners who don't have many flowers, but they may lead you into temptation. They're deep enough for two layers of flowers, which is a sacred no-no that I ignore all the time.

When to pick?

The best time to pick flowers for drying is the worst time to pick flowers for arranging—i.e., in the middle of a hot, sunny day. You don't want them dripping with morning dew or raindrops. It's only common sense to start with the driest flowers possible, but it isn't fatal to bend this rule, either. If you feel in your bones that a hurricane's on the way, dash on out at midnight and pick your precious marigolds.

That brings up another question. Do you have to carry your trusty water bucket when you're picking flowers for drying? You bet you do. You have to pick your flowers at their peak and keep them at their peak till the very last minute. In fact, expert Georgia O. Vance even recommends conditioning them—that is, soaking them up to their chins overnight. (Don't worry about the wet stems—they get snipped off anyway.) The point is that you can't turn a droopy fresh flower into a sparkling dried flower. It simply won't get better looking, like Joe Namath, every day.

When is a flower at its peak? Usually, just when you think it is. Pick zinnias and marigolds, for instance, in full bloom, just when you'd pick them for arranging. But many flowers will continue to open while drying, so it's better to err on the early side than the late. Three important exceptions are strawflowers, blue salvia, and goldenrod, which should be picked while one-third or more still in bud. When you pick is as important as what you pick, and you'll find detailed charts in many flower-drying books. Be sure to include some buds in your pickings, too. Garden clubbers love buds, and I've found that rosebuds, for one, hold up better than full-blown blooms. (If your roses are already shot, you can turn them into "buds" by stripping off the damaged outer petals.)

What next?

Most flower stems go to pieces when dry, so you have to add wire stems. First snip your flower stem one or two inches from the top and remove all foliage; then poke a short piece of No. 24 florist's wire just into the head of the flower. For heavier flowers such as zinnias and marigolds, bend the wire into a hook at the top and pull it down firmly. Prewiring your flowers is, admittedly, a pain in the neck, but you'll hate yourself if you put it off. It's ten times tougher at the arranging end of the operation.

Most flowers are dried face up. Flat, single-petaled flowers like daisies go face down. A few others, like delphiniums, are placed horizontally. In any case, the idea is to bury the flower completely in sand—but slowly, gently, lovingly. Sift the sand through your fingers so that it gets between each petal, or use a handled tin cup.

Finish up with an even, all-covering layer, move the box to a dry place, and forget about it. If you're over forty years old and losing fifty thousand memory cells per day, label each box with the date and the kind of flower. Most flowers take between one and two weeks to dry, depending on the variety and the drying conditions. The best way to tell is to sample one or two; if they feel dry, they probably are. Don't despair if they slip your mind for weeks on end. The flowers won't be as bright, but they'll probably turn out okay.

The finishing touches

Chances are you'll be wildly proud of your first batch of flowers just as is. But you can gussy them up even more. Dust off the excess sand with a small artist's brush. Use a dampened brush if particles are stubborn. Another crazy-sounding but effective clean-up method is what Georgia Vance calls sand blasting. Simply pour a steady stream of new sand, from a height of about one foot, to remove old sand from the flowers.

Now you're ready to finish your stems. Overlap a long piece of No. 24 wire onto the short, wired end of the flower and wrap with floral tape. The trick here is to get a good, tight start. Then twist the tape between your right thumb and forefinger as your left hand pulls down hard. Snip off the end to leave a sharp tip to insert into your styrofoam or whatever.

What to pick

A complete list of flowers suitable for sand drying would read like the Wayside Gardens catalog. You'll find such lists in the books in your library, but here are a few old-faithfuls to cut your teeth on.

Start with "Lemon Drop" marigolds. Lemon Drop is the first flower I ever dried, the flower that convinced me I was a flower-drying genius, and the only flower I still dry every year no matter what. Lemon Drop is the little French marigold that's always the brightest, lemoniest, yellowest flower in anybody's garden. You can buy anything from seeds to full potted plants, but flats of seedlings are cheap and ubiquitous. In Maryland gardens, Lemon Drop is more likely to self-seed than not, and a starter flat can provide you with bountiful golden clumps for years. It isn't *quite* so brilliant dried as it is in the garden, but a merry bunch in a copper bowl or Delft pitcher could cheer you up all winter. (Large marigolds are also dryable, but mine always look as though they've been sat on.)

Another surefire dryer is zinnia. All types of zinnias, except curly or ruffled kinds, dry well—provided you're not fussy about color. Yellow zinnias may turn pale or golden. Orange zinnias may turn pink. White turns beige. Deep oranges and reds tend to "gray" or turn almost black. My favorite zinnia for drying is salmon pink Lilliput (it stays salmon-pink). Lilliput is the bushy, button-type zinnia that's also called "Cut-and-Come-Again" and that everybody gets mixed up with Thumbelina. Don't buy Thumbelina by mistake—it's the dwarf type used for edging.

Zinnias come in every color you could ask for, except blue. If you want blue dried flowers, remember that practically all of

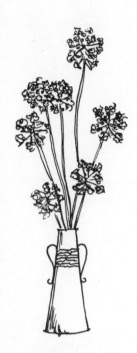

them are washouts but three of them are knockouts. The ones you want are delphinium, ageratum, and blue salvia (which can also be air dried). If you want white-white flowers, not creamy-white, try daisies, deutzia, delphinium, or feverfew.

Some other good bets are black-eyed Susans, single dahlias, open-throat snapdragons, physostegia (false dragonhead), tithonia, and oenothera (evening primrose). If the list seems short, it's because most garden flowers dry even better in silica gel than in sand, and many favorites can be air dried.

Of course, Queen Anne's lace isn't a garden flower. It's a weed (you read about it in Chapter 3). But it's probably the most beautiful dried flower of all. It's certainly the most beautiful *free* flower. Dried in ordinary sand, it looks almost as fresh as the real thing. Queen Anne's lace is an indispensable filler in mixed dried bouquets. It's enchanting with Christmas greens—the flat, starry flower heads look like delicate white snowflakes perched among the leaves. Or use it all by its elegant self, soaring proudly on dried day-lily stems. (Lee Radziwill hangs it in wicker baskets.)

For the whitest flower, pick Queen Anne's lace before it's three-fourths open, but be sure to pick some overripe "bird's nest" pods, too. For a change of pace, dye it pink or yellow or green. Simply add food coloring to the water and let stand overnight.

Here are some common flowers *not* worth fooling with: petunia, poppy, peony, impatiens, day lily, iris, and geranium. But you don't have to take my word for it, any more than my gardening-nut brother-in-law did. I told him not to break his heart drying chrysanthemums, and guess what I got for Christmas? A dried chrysanthemum.

Silica is quicka

If you think sand-dried flowers are nifty, wait till you try silica gel. Once you've dried flowers in silica gel, you may never use sand again. Silica gel is a powdery white chemical compound that's lighter than sand, feels nicer than sand, works faster than sand, and dries flowers twice as bright as sand. There's only one hitch—silica gel costs money. One of the most popular makes, Flower-Dri, costs $4.25 for one and a half pounds, and $9.95 for four pounds. You can forget the small can—it's not enough to dry a fly. Even four pounds doesn't go far once you get the drying bug. But there's one consolation—silica gel can be used over and over again. Once it's yours, it's yours forever. Why, you can will it to your grandchildren. (Flower-Dri and other compounds are sold in garden-supply stores, most florists', and many hardware and department stores. They tell me you can make your own if you have a pet chemical-supply house. Ask for five pounds of 28-200 mesh crystals of silica gel and one pound of 6-16 Tel-Tale crystals.)

Silica-gel drying is just like sand drying, except for two things. One, you have to watch your timing. Most flowers are "done" in three to four days, and when they're done, they're done. If you cook them any longer, they'll shrink, burn, or turn brittle. Two— and here's where the hassle comes in—flowers in silica gel have to be sealed absolutely airtight. That means you need all the cake and cookie tins you can round up. If you don't have VIP friends who get twenty-five fruit cakes at Christmas, try the thrift shops. Shiny new tins at the dime store are much too extravagant. You can also use wide-mouthed jars or coffee cans with lids, but cake tins are bigger and better.

Hot from the oven

Ah, at last we come to my whole reason for writing this book: to tell the world about baked daffodils. That's right, *baked*, right in your oven. Of course, you don't bake daffodils in their skins like potatoes; you bake them in a tin of silica gel, left uncovered this time. You use your lowest setting—150 to 180 degrees, or "warm." They take twelve to eighteen hours, which isn't exactly Sara Lee–speedy, but it's still much faster than sand. That's the whole secret of silica gel's success. The longer it takes to dry a flower, the paler and wanner it gets. Sand is so-so because it takes weeks. Silica gel is better because it takes days. Silica gel in the oven is supersensational because it takes mere hours.

It may be just common sense, but to me a brilliant bright yellow baked daffodil is a miracle. So are baked tulips (18 to 24 hours), baked hyacinths (24 hours), and baked peonies (24 hours). Some other temperamental flowers to bake are camellias, chrysanthemums, pansies, and roses. According to most experts, roses aren't tricky at all and can be sand dried along with zinnias and marigolds. But I've never seen a sand-dried rose that can compare with my dazzling orange-red baked "Tropicanas" (14 to 16 hours). And I can't wait to try anemones (12 to 18 hours).

Before you find out the hard way, let me warn you that baking anything for 18 hours poses problems. Say you start your flowers bright and early at ten in the morning—you'll have to set your alarm for four o'clock the next morning. Forget it! So how about cooking them from 3 in the afternoon till nine the next morning? Swell, except how do you cook the family's dinner? If every time your husband asks what's in the oven, you answer "Daffodils!" you'll soon be cooking for one. One exhausting solution is to start the operation after you've finished the dinner dishes, but I've found an easier out. Simply take the flowers out while the biscuits or roast are in and finish cooking them later. But do keep track of your ins and outs—eighteen hours is a long time to remember anything.

Baked daffodils have certain fringe benefits, too. They make good party talk when the other girls are swapping zucchini recipes. "Baked *what?*" I even startled my mother-in-law, who I'd have sworn was unflappable by now. When I told her I was baking daffodils, she gulped and asked weakly, "Do the *children* eat them, too?" And they're superb for getting rid of long-winded telephoners. By the time your friends recover from "Oops, gotta go—I have daffodils in the oven," you'll be off and running.

(P.S.: Insert your wired daffodils into hollow day-lily stems or even painted paper straws. Fudge with skinny iris leaves—they usually dry better than daffodil foliage.)

Out of thin air

Air drying is the easiest method of all, and the only method used by the persnickety Williamsburg people. Which may explain why Williamsburg bouquets are so wishy-washy (beautiful, to be sure, but no pizazz). I don't mean that all air-dried flowers are dull. Strawflowers are as bright and zingy as you could ask for,

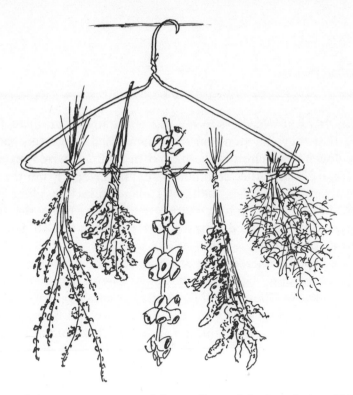

although I suspect commercial suppliers of dyeing theirs. Chinese lanterns and bittersweet keep their orange; celosia and dock keep their red; baby's breath *sometimes* holds its white; blue salvia stays surprisingly blue; yarrow and goldenrod stay yellow enough. But these are the exceptions, and I can't stand celosia. Or yarrow, as a garden flower—I grow it in an out-of-the-way corner just to dry. One of my good friends and neighbors tried for years to give me yarrow, along with a bunch of the other gifties that make my garden what it is today. After I discovered flower drying, I took her up on it and have blessed her ever since.

Generally, the best reason for air-drying flowers is laziness. In Williamsburg they have proper drying rooms in the attic, hung with black cloth, where flowers can "mature in isolation and darkness" like fine wines. But all you really need is a clothesline in the basement or a few inches in a dark closet. To prepare your flowers, just strip off the leaves (with a gardening glove or old oven mitt you can swoosh down the stems in seconds). Tie the stems in small bunches with twist-ems and hang them upside down from the clothesline or wire hanger.

You can also dry some flowers, like hydrangeas, standing up. Late-blooming white *Hydrangea paniculata* is best. (You'll see it pictured at the beginning of Chapter 13.) Pick it in every stage from cream to chartreuse to pink to beige; heap it in a basket and enjoy it while it dries. Many field gatherings, such as marsh grass, corn tassels, and milkweed, will take on even more interesting curves that way. Needless to say, one of the joys of air-dried flowers is that they can stand on their own dried stems (except for strawflowers, which must be picked in bud and wired pronto).

Here are some other common plants to air-dry. From the garden: artemisia, baptisia, bells of Ireland, feverfew, globe amaranth, honesty, red salvia, statice, and tansy. From the field: boneset, butterfly weed, cattail, pearly everlasting, sumac, and wild mustard.

I hope you wondered what all those gaudy *flowers* were doing on the cover of a book about flower arranging without flowers. Now you know. Those aren't flower-flowers; they're dried flowers —all home-grown (except for the wildlings), and home-dried in either sand, silica gel, or thin air. I'm sinfully proud of them, of course, but I have to admit that the bouquet is four years old; we don't have central air-conditioning; we do have a wood-burning fireplace; and over the moons the sun has taken its toll. If you want to see truly brilliant flowers, you should see Georgia Vance's, the expert I've already mentioned. I first saw Mrs. Vance's miracle flowers at a GCA workshop back in 1969 when she was arranging flowers for the State Department in Washington. Luckily for you, she's since written a book about it: *The Decorative Art of Dried Flower Arrangement*, Doubleday, 1972.

Ever (and ever) greens

What did I say away back when about long-winded experts? But you must have leaves to go with your flowers. In a nutshell, there are four main ways to preserve foliage.

To glycerinize leaves (such as magnolia, laurel, eucalyptus, forsythia), first slit and pound the stems about two inches up. Stand them in about four inches of one part glycerin to two parts water until the solution reaches the tips of the leaves, usually about two weeks. Glycerin is sold in drugstores and isn't cheap. For a poor girl's substitute, snitch some of your husband's antifreeze.

To press leaves (such as fern, ivy, and silver poplar), place them between several sheets of newspaper and weight them with books or rocks, or slip them under the rug. Wipe them lightly with cooking oil first to keep them supple. Change the papers after a few days to keep them greener. Leaves dry in about one month but can stay put for many more. You can dry whole dogwood, beech, or oak branches, while still full of sap, in newspaper under boards.

The *evaporation method* is a good way to preserve exotic houseplant leaves such as orchid, rubber plant, and aspidistra. Simply place them on absorbent paper for two to three weeks, turning them over occasionally. They'll curl into their own interesting shapes. Hosta leaves from the garden and mullein leaves from the field are other possibilities. Dry pussy willow and berried nandina branches with no water in the container, but for some reason boxwood likes to dry out "wet." Leave a little water in the container to dry up gradually. A forgotten spray of flowering andromeda turned gorgeous shades of red, cream, and mahogany by this method, eventually ending up a rich tan.

Sand drying, which you know all about, works fine with rose leaves, peony leaves, ivy, vines, and ferns such as maidenhair and Baker's. Incidentally, if you're perpetually fresh out of fern, as I am, try making do with Queen Anne's lace foliage.

Drying flowers in ivory towers

If you're an apartment dweller, you've probably been decorating with gaudy strawflowers and gloomy lotus pods year after year, just like every other girl in town. But, happily, dried materials are finally coming into their own. More and more city florists are rearranging their furniture to make room for fascinating live-forevers—dried flowers, dried leaves, pods, cones, and of course driftwood. And most big cities have at least one kooky shop that sells nothing but dried doodads. You should have no trouble finding statice, starflowers, celosia, yarrow, baby's breath, artemisia, sea lavender, artichokes, manzanita, Scotch broom, and spiral eucalyptus. You'll probably have your pick of dried grasses and grains (Ali MacGraw likes wheat stalk centerpieces) as well as dried palm or palmetto leaves. So-called wood roses (actually the seed pod of Hawaiian morning glory) have been around for years, and exotic African wood daisies are popping up everywhere.

But that's the trouble with dried things in the city—they're so all-fired exotic. You can find dozens of unusual, intriguing imports from the four corners of the earth, but not one little born-free buttercup or bunch of humble Queen Anne's lace. The only way a city girl can buy plain old, pretty old dried garden flowers is in an already made arrangement—at an outrageous price. Even the teeniest mini-bouquet may cost $8 or $10. And it's probably dyed at that. One New York City specialist does "natural-looking" custom arrangements (his flowers, your heirloom teacup) that start at $15. But that's just for starters—on Manhattan's affluent East Side, dried arrangements cost up to $1000. And you're still getting only pods and starflowers—not roses and daffodils and tulips in a full-blown garden bouquet.

Sorry, I almost forgot—you *can* buy boxes of loose dried flowers to arrange yourself. They're made by the Eighteenth Century Bouquet Company of Princeton, New Jersey, and are sold everywhere including the Craft House in Williamsburg, for shame). Still no roses or daffodils, but the flowers are bright and pretty and come in red, gold, pink, pastel, and mixed shades. Are you ready for the price? Fourteen-fifty for the small box, $22.75 for the medium, and $31.00 for the large (with quotes around *large*). No wonder they nearly slipped my mind. As the sales copy says reassuringly, you can "limit your florist bill with a box of these to last season after season," but I have an even thriftier idea. Dry your own.

Who, you? Why not? Basically, drying florist's flowers is no different from drying garden flowers. The main difference is psychological. You'll remember that garden flowers must be picked and dried at their peak. The same goes for florist's flowers. In other words, when you splurge on a dozen roses for drying, you can't sit around sniffing them for a week. You've got to buy them and bury them, one-two-three. That takes more steely sangfroid than many girls can muster, but try to think of the long, rosy years ahead. Or dry only two or three roses at a time.

Roses, of course, are the wildest splurge you'll have to rationalize. There are lots of cheaper flowers you can dry—daisies, snapdragons, dahlias, tulips, daffodils, hyacinths, heather, gladioli, and lilies of the valley. I'd be leery of drying supermarket daffo-

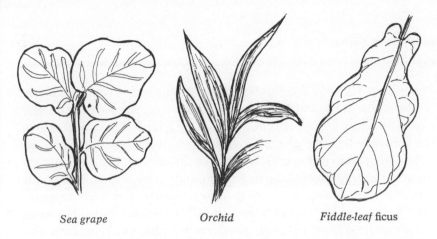

Sea grape　　　　　*Orchid*　　　　　*Fiddle-leaf* ficus

dils, but if you want to try them, how much can you lose? Generally, I'd suggest using silica gel. It's more available to city girls than sand is, and you might as well get the best, brightest results for your money.

By all means, dry your own florist's leaves, too. Magnolia, lemon, galax, eucalyptus, podocarpus, beech, and leatherleaf fern all do well in glycerin. Palm, ti, canna, rubber, calla lily, bird-of-paradise, and Scotch broom can be hung to dry or dried standing up in a container. Try twisting spiky leaves around a stick to dry in interesting spirals. Leaves of orchid, sea grape, cecropia, croton, and fiddle-leaf *ficus* take on graceful shapes through the evaporation method. Florists also sell fresh berries which you can dry, such as bittersweet and rose-colored pepper berries from California. And don't overlook fresh branches, both flowering and non-.

As I've said before, the fields and meadows are just as free to city girls as to country girls, if farther-flung. The next time you venture off the concrete, don't come home empty-handed. You don't need binoculars to spot fields of goldenrod, black-eyed Susans, daisies, and Queen Anne's lace. You can't miss tall, flaming tiger lilies, either. (The flowers don't dry well, but the long hollow stems are good for holding up other dried flowers.) If you can't see keeping a water bucket in the car, bring along some plastic bags filled with wet newspaper to keep your gatherings fresh.

There's one flower that separates city girls from country girls— baby's breath. Sure, florists sell baby's breath, both fresh and dried, but they sell it like diamonds on stems. What good are a few measly overpriced sprigs? You want clouds and clouds of the beautiful stuff. You want it to fill in and puff out a mixed bouquet. You want it to poke into enchanting mini-arrangements. You want it to heap lavishly, all by itself, into an elegant silver champagne bucket as in the illustration at the beginning of the chapter.

Unfortunately, baby's breath is hard to come by even in the country. Only one of my good gardening friends, bless her, grows it successfully. I've given up, because it either doesn't come up at all or crowds out everything else in the garden. But the country is still the only place you can afford to buy it by the armful. You'll find bargain bunches of dried baby's breath at church bazaars, garden-club sales, and occasionally offbeat flower shops. If I were a city girl, I'd leave a standing order with suburban friends to buy for two whenever they spot it (and offer some city-chic lotus pods in exchange).

The care and feeding of dried flowers

The first year you get into flower drying, you won't have any storage problem. You'll have your handiwork on display all over the house. Your only problem will be summer safekeeping for arrangements. (Quick, before the humidity gets them, pop them into plastic bags, seal tight, and tuck into a safe corner.)

But wait till next year. What do you do with three dozen dried zinnias, eighty-nine marigolds, and six priceless "Queen Elizabeth" roses? Short of adding an extra air-conditioned wing to the house, there's no easy way to store dried flowers. Just finding enough boxes to put them in is challenge enough. If you're ambitious, you can build floor-to-ceiling shelves and line up your flowers in neatly labeled and tightly sealed jars. Some people prefer stacks of dress boxes. I like hat boxes. Hat boxes hold a lot, are easy to seal with masking tape, and look more glamorous than other boxes, so are less likely to get shoved around. The best place to find hat boxes is the thrift shop, but some dime stores sell them, too. I don't know what other people buy hat boxes for, but apparently they don't buy them like hotcakes—I always get mine at half price.

Line the box with cotton or shredded wax paper and add a spoonful or two of silica gel. Stand extra-special flowers in a cake of styrofoam. Seal the box with masking tape and store in a sealed plastic bag (giant trash bags will accommodate an assortment of hat boxes, shoe boxes, et cetera). Don't forget to label each box, preferably before it's sealed and you've forgotten what's inside.

To protect dried flowers in an arrangement, spray them with artist's acrylic spray or even plain hair spray. To freshen straw-flowers or celosia, hold them over a pot of steam. I've heard that you can revive a dusty arrangement by (1) spraying it with a fine mist of water; (2) blowing it with a hairdryer; or (3) sucking the dust in with a vacuum cleaner, but I for one have never had the guts to try.

Pressed but not prissy

I am not, repeat *not*, going to tell you how to make pressed-flower pictures. Go to the library, please. I'm not even going to tell you how to press flowers. Not properly, that is. I learned from an expert's expert, and the proper pressing of flowers is too fussy-Mary for me. The way I see it, pressing flowers should be fun; and the way I do it, it is. Just drop your flowers between sheets of newspaper and slip them under a rug. By my method, it doesn't matter how many weeks, months, or years go by before you think of them again. They'll wait for you and look surprisingly red, yellow, or blue, as the case may be. They may not be the same color they were to begin with, but they'll be *some* color (blues turn lavender, for instance).

I bring up pressed flowers on the chance that you're as tired as I am of cutesie-poo pansies and forget-me-nots framed in gold and strung on velvet ribbons. Isn't there anything else you can do with pressed flowers? Isn't there some way to fit them into a 1970s decor? Yes, there is.

For one thing, you can use weeds and grasses instead of sweet verbena. Better still, you can invent your own flowers. There's no need to frame flowers just as they grow. Take them apart. Press a bunch of bright pink zinnia *petals* or gaudy fringed gaillardia petals and reassemble them with the center of another flower. Or drop a whole buttercup or viola into the middle. (Actually, there's no other way to press fat, chunky flowers but petal by petal.) Save the calyx of an iris, carnation, or dahlia and press it for a you-name-it flower. Or forget about flowers altogether and compose a far-out abstract design with your pressed materials.

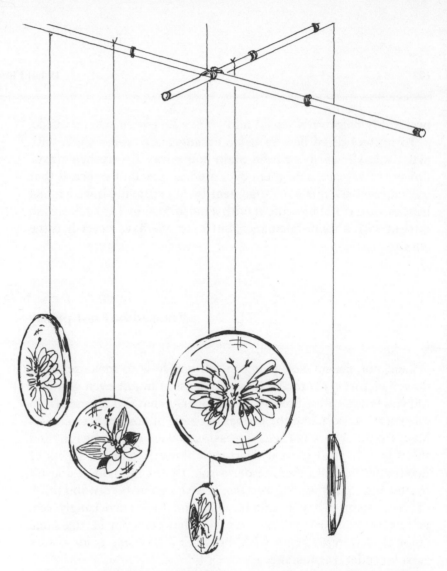

My first "contemporary" effort was a free-form floral pressed between two sheets of Plexiglas and bound with tape. I scattered giant white pansies, blue chicory found in a sidewalk crack, and houseplant fern willy-nilly, and—well, at least it didn't look "eighteenth century." In fact, it looked quite mod dangling in a sunny window. You can get the same effect, cheaper, with laminated plastic sheets. Or try a carefree composition under the glass top of a dressing table.

My next experiment was a so-called arrangement for a placement flower show. A placement show is held in a private home, with each exhibitor assigned a particular spot to enhance—mantelpiece, dining room table, bedside chest, et cetera. The show had a theatrical theme, and my place was on the "Anything Goes" patio. Instead of a bona fide bouquet, I fudged with a mobile called Butterflies Are Free. The butterflies were petals of hot-

orange and pink zinnias, flaming tithonia, and bright blue delphinium embedded in clear plastic resin. (No, it didn't win the
blue ribbon, but it took the judges all day to make up their
minds.)

From dangling plastic discs it was a short step to sitting plastic
trivets. By now pressed-flower trivets are all over the place, but,
immodestly, I lay claim to blazing the trail. If you'd rather make
your own trivet than pay $10 or $12 for a store-bought model with
cheap dyed flowers and tired fern, all you need is a can of Clear-
Cast liquid plastic, an old bowl for a mold, and a clothespin (the
stuff smells terrible). You'll find Clear-Cast (American Handi-
crafts) and directions for using it in craft and art-supply stores.
If you're really lazy, try my own exclusive see-through coasters.
Pour a layer of plastic into tin lids (mine came with a jelly-
making set). In about half an hour, add your pressed flowers and
cover with more plastic. When casting is hard, remove from mold
(a brief warmup in the oven makes the job easier). Instead of the
usual smattering of pansies, try one "snowflake" of Queen Anne's
lace. Twice the elegance and half the work.

Grab bag of flower-drying tips

- Light-colored flowers (pinks, yellows, oranges) dry the
truest.
- The best pink roses to dry are "Queen Elizabeth" and "Royal
Highness."
- Lilacs can be made more purple by shaking them in a bag
along with powdered chalk.
- Lily of the valley can be whitened by spraying with Accent
floral paint (Illinois Bronze Powder & Paint Company).
- Any dried material can be given a dramatic new look with
a coat of paint (how about white iris leaves or bright green wild
sumac?).
- Grains and grasses should be sprayed with two coats of clear
spray to preserve them.
- Globe thistle should be picked before it blooms, globe amaranth after it blooms.

- Pearly everlasting should be picked in bud (when you see the little yellow dot in the tip).
- Gladioli can be picked after the first frost for a naturally dried, pale beige flower.
- Sweet gum branches should be cut before frost to retain their red color in glycerin.
- Roses can be glued together (before drying) with thinned Elmer's glue applied sparingly to the bases of the petals.
- Zinnias and marigolds can be glued together (after drying) with Elmer's glue.
- Mums and dahlias can be sprayed (from the back) with a waxlike fixative called Candle-Mum.
- Rosettes of pachysandra steeped in antifreeze will turn from greenish bronze to clear, lovely yellow.
- As flowers in your fresh bouquets (roses, carnations, delphinium, anemones, rose leaves, lemon geranium, lemon verbena) begin to dry out, hang or spread them in an airy place for the beginning of a great potpourri.

Part Two

How to Flower-Arrange
on a Shoestring

8

Put Your Flowers Where They'll Count the Most

EVERY GOOD HOUSEWIFE KNOWS how to stretch a pound of hamburger to feed twenty drop-in guests. (You send out for Gin Gon Loon Ha.) But what do you know about str-r-retching flowers? Can you turn one lonely flower into an arrangement? Can you make two flowers look like a dozen and a dozen like a whole houseful? It's easier than you think. In fact, it's a whole lot easier than food stretching, and much less obvious. You'll never fool anybody with your clever noodle-padded casserole, but you could fool your mother-in-law with a padded flower arrangement.

For one thing, most people aren't used to fresh flowers in a house. They're utterly ho-hum about wall-to-wall broadloom, built-in bars, and color TV, but they're downright dumbstruck by real, honest-to-Burpee unplastic flowers. So, it doesn't take many to impress them, bless them. For another thing, most people don't really *look* at flower arrangements. Do you? Unless all your friends are flower-show judges, nobody's going to poke her nose into your peonies or count the daisies in your centerpiece. Most people don't know one flower from another, anyway. All you need is a bunch of something here and a bunch of something else there, and everyone will think you have flowers, flowers everywhere. If your "flowers" are chockful of Hyacinth Helper, no one will ever know but poor-but-clever you.

Hey, you forgot my greens

The oldest, and still the best, flower stretcher of all is greens. Or did you think greens were "out"? True, it's a sin to ruin a dozen American Beauty roses with clouds of tacky asparagus fern, but even the florists have finally realized that there are other greens in the world.

These days, when you open your box of roses, you're likely to find huckleberry leaves, podocarpus, lemon leaves, or lycopodium. Only a ninny would throw goodies like these in the garbage. Certainly no garden clubber would. Garden clubbers always use greens in their arrangements, and not because they're short of flowers. They use them because they want to win blue ribbons. Greens are "in," so use every precious scrap in the box. You may end up with two or three gorgeous arrangements instead of just one (no matter how many flowers you have, they're still worth stretching). In the chapter frontispiece, five roses are stretched into a queen-size arrangement with podocarpus. The "vase" is a spray-can cap attached to an old plate, both sprayed black.

But suppose nobody sent you roses this week. When *you're* at the florist's doing the buying, it's even sillier to snub giveaway greens. Be sure you get all that are coming to you. If the florist is absent-minded, nudge him. If he's stingy, smile—he may throw in some extras. Let him know how you feel about greens (greedy). Don't be afraid to ask him what kinds he has today or coax him into letting you take a look for yourself out back.

Naturally, if you're only buying three carnations you won't stagger out with freebie greens. You may even have to buy some. In that case, you needn't be so smily. You can be downright choosy. As long as you're paying, you may as well get good, fresh greens that will solve your flower-stretching problem for weeks and weeks.

Take them; they're yours

If you're a country girl your problem isn't finding good, fresh greens—it's learning to use them. Some of the brightest gardeners I know are still in the dark about greens. They'll use daffodil leaves with their daffodils and peony leaves with peonies, but that's as far as their imagination goes. Wise old arrangers use every green leaf they can put their hands on. They borrow leaves from one flower to use with another. They use leaves from flowers that have finished blooming. They use leaves from pretty plants that most people just sit and look at—ornamentals like hosta, sedum, and coleus. They take clippings from ordinary evergreens, like pine, hemlock, and yew. They take snippings from their pride-and-joys, like holly, azalea, euonymus, aucuba, and nandina (if I just lost you, go back to Chapter 1—it's all about greens).

And don't forget about the next-best real-live fillers you've learned about—branches, weeds, fruits and vegetables, dried flowers, and houseplants. All you need are two tulips and a bough of apple blossoms, or one lily and a bowl of oranges. With an armful of wild Queen Anne's lace, you can turn three zinnias into a buxom, full-blown bouquet. And think of all the autumn gatherings you can use to pad out a few precious mums. (City girls can do their "nature walking" at street stands in the fall.)

Figurines, fungi, and other fillips

Do you have any knickknacks around the house? Everybody has knickknacks around the house. Why not use them in your arrangements the way garden clubbers do? One teakwood Buddha or porcelain bluebird can take up a lot of room in a flower bowl. In fact, in many flower-show designs the figurine is practically the whole arrangement, with maybe a few leaves in back and a couple of flowers in front. But, especially in a centerpiece, be sure you really like the figurine or knickknack if you're going to make your guests look at it all through dinner. To tell the truth, I'd rather look at a fine fungus any day than most people's figurines. It's not fancy *objets d'art* but plain old objects that are the backbone of flower arranging these days.

Almost any "found" object is "in"—an interesting rock, a nice piece of coal, a hunk of quartz, a tangled root, a chunk of coral, a slab of bark. Seashells have always been big in flower-arranging circles, and, needless to say, one piece of driftwood is worth a thousand glads. You can also fill up your bowl with polished stones and pebbles. But you don't even need a bowl. Hairdresser Vidal Sassoon strews a handful of burnished black stones and highly polished apples on a bright red cloth and calls it a centerpiece.

Another favorite of the pros is colored glass chips. Scatter them lavishly over a large, shallow crystal platter, add water to make them sparkle even more, and all you need are three pretty posies in one corner. Stand them in a pinholder and camouflage it with glossy green leaves. Add a few drops of food coloring for fun. You can buy glass chips at fancy prices in gift shops, but don't. Use colored pebbles from the tropical fish department; or, better still, round up all your old bottles and start smashing. (Use several double-strength grocery bags and a good hammer.)

You won't believe all the weird and wondrous things garden clubbers come up with. One woman borrowed a filter from her oil burner and won a blue ribbon. Others build masterpieces around a clump of barnacles, an old stove pipe, or a holey plastic carrier from a six-pack. Serious arrangers have so many treasures in their basements, attics, and garages that they're embarrassed to call in a repairman. They gather them here, there, and everywhere, and if nobody knows what they *are*, so much the better. Even old pros don't know every oddity that lurks in woods, fields,

thrift shops and junkyards. I have some bleached kelp roots that stump everyone—my sister-in-law found them on a secret beach in California. I wouldn't trade them for a dozen black orchids. In short, there's more to flower arranging than flowers from the florist. As the ribbon-winningest woman I know says when they ask her how she does it, "I keep my eyes open."

Candlelight and wiles

Everybody knows that candles and flowers go together, but the question is, how do you put them together? Do you always plunk your candles, one-two, to the left and right of your center-piece? What a waste. Try planting them smack in the middle of it. There's nothing sexier than a few random tapers flickering among the freesias. And you won't need half as many freesias. Instead of a mostly flowers bouquet with candles growing out of it, try a mostly candles bouquet. Set tall candles of varying heights in the corner of a low bowl and add a handful of pretty blooms at the base. Or set your flowers adrift on cork floats, usually sold in garden-supply stores. Have you discovered Flambuoyants yet?

They're clear plastic discs that, filled with salad oil, will float and flicker for twenty-four hours in any water-filled container.

How do you make candles stand up in a bowl of water? The secret is a special candle attachment that fits snugly into your pinholder. Another idea for candles-plus-flowers is to cut a hole in a round of styrofoam and slip the ring about halfway down a tall taper (you'll have to use long-lasting flowers like daisies or mums, stay-fresh greens, or fake flowers). Or simply set a chunky candle on a compote and add a few posies or leaves. Line up or group several of these—the compotes don't have to match (or make your own as in Chapter 13).

Flower shops sell another tricky flower-arranging attachment designed for branched candelabra. It's an Oasis-filled round container that fits into the hole where a candle usually goes. Add a few geraniums, geranium leaves, and tendrils of ivy, and your table will be all aglow and all abloom at the same time.

And remember the old-fashioned pansy ring? It's perfect for a flowery nimbus around a grouping of candles or one big fat one. I found this nifty, new-fangled arranger in a New York shop over

ten years ago and I have no idea if they still make them (Center-piece Flower Arranger, Inc., White Plains, N.Y.). It's a nine-inch clear plastic ring with a lift-out top riddled with assorted-size holes (seventy-six, to be exact, just like trombones). The beauty of it is that you can use flowers with short stems, long stems or no stems. And the arranging time? Five minutes flat, including picking time.

Incidentally, if you have any kind of pansy ring, you don't have to stick to pansies. Tuck in a piece of everything you've got—a single white petunia, a snippet of coralbells, a spray of blue salvia, a sprig of purplish basil or any other herb, and certainly lots of shy little wildlings. And don't forget to use smidgins of oversized common flowers. Two or three gaudy florets of geranium, delphinium, or hydrangea, for instance, will have everybody wondering what on earth your exotic miniatures can be.

Surprise, surprise

So much for tangible, flesh-and-blood flower stretchers. Now let's get psychological. Have you ever gone to a party and found an anemone—one perfect, dewy, fresh-cut anemone—blooming in the john? Would you ever forget it if you had? Would you doubt for one minute that your hostess was flower-people? That's what I call psychological flower-stretching.

The idea is to put your flowers where they'll count the most. You could spend $20 on a dining room centerpiece and nobody would even blink an eye or remember it two days later. Everybody has flowers on the dinner table. You're expected to have flowers on the dinner table. But put a 75¢ anemone in an unexpected place and you'll be famous.

Think of some other surprising places for flowers—it's easy and fun. With all of today's swinging do-your-own-thinging, most people are still complete fuddy-duds about flowers. They put flowers where people have always put flowers—on the coffee table, on the piano, and in the front hall. In other words, you don't have go far far out to be different. You don't have to have lilies hanging from the chandelier, sweet peas blooming in Fido's water bowl, or gerberas tucked behind the sofa cushions (another uninhibited Sassoon notion). All you need is a dollop of derring-do.

How about flowers on the floor? The nice thing about floor flowers is that you don't have to arrange them—they look *better* just dumped into an ice bucket, wood box, or umbrella stand. And you don't have to worry about table space—pick any spot in the room where they'll make a splash. One of the best spots is the hearth. Maybe flames aren't the best thing in the world for flowers, but there's nothing more lavishly Hollywoodish than a tub of bright fresh flowers by a roaring open fire. In the summer, put your flowers *in* the fireplace (along with a fresh coat of paint). Of course, you can use dried flowers instead. Or try a basket of huge, gaudy paper flowers on the floor of your powder room.

How about flowers in the bookcase? Japanese homes have a special niche called a *tokonoma* for arrangements, but all you need is a cleared-off space on the shelf. Why not flowers on a stair landing, or even balanced on the banister? Why not flowers *underneath* a glass table? Do you have a precious don't-sit-on-me antique chair? Perfect.

If you've never used your mantel because it's too skinny for a conventional bouquet, line up a row of little bouquets. Use your mirrors to create a visual effect of double bouquets. And, by all

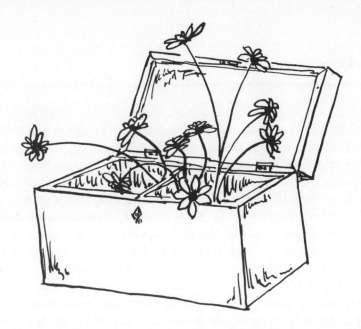

means, perch nonchalant see-through arrangements on the sill of your picture window. Department stores sell a clear acrylic stepladder designed expressly to hold houseplants and bouquets. It's thirty-nine inches high and costs $15. (I've also seen a miniature version only twelve inches high for the same price. It must be a super grade of acrylic!) But why not use an ordinary shiny aluminum ladder or brightly painted "antique"?

Party, party

How many years have you put your party flowers in the same old vase on the same old cocktail table? This time, scatter them around. Let your guests stumble on a cluster of bright-eyed daisies in an antique tea caddy over here and a few shy violets peeking out of a silver cigarette box over there. Even one iris or two roses or three lilies is an arrangement, as you'll see in Chapter 9.

Another brilliant way to make the most of what you've got is to color-key your flowers to a painting overhead or to the fabric on a nearby chair. Three anemones in pink, red, and purple might do the trick. Or, if you have a yellow and orange painting over the mantel, drop a cache pot of yellow flowers to one side and a basket of orange ones to the other. A favorite poor-girl arrangement on our pink, orange, and purple patio is a handful of purple iris and wild orange lilies in a pink and green watermelon "bowl." Or color-key your flowers to the container. Bright red flowers in a bright red container make a smashing splash. Incidentally, even if you settle for the same old mixed bouquet in your favorite old vase, don't settle for the same old spotty, wishy-washy mishmash of colors. Bunch together all the yellows, pinks, purples, and reds —they'll have more zing. (**P.S.**: It's smart to use the same flowers again and again if they're the *only* flowers you ever use. Let lilies or daisies become your trademark and you won't need more than a handful. Your guests will go looking for them like the rabbit on the cover of *Playboy*.)

And on party night you can be sure that your front rooms aren't the only rooms your guests will see. Don't forget flowers on the bar, even if the bar is only your kitchen counter. Do a "fruit-and-vegetable" arrangement for the breakfast table. Wouldn't nosegays in the children's rooms make their eyes pop? How about flowers by the telephone, where everyone's bound to see them? How about flowers *outside* the house? A door arrangement may seem like a terrible waste of flowers, but think of the stunning first—and last—impression it will make on your guests. (That goes double for apartment dwellers.)

The rubber two-dollar bill

To get back to that twenty-dollar dinner-table centerpiece that nobody will remember two days later but everybody expects. What's a poor girl to do? You can't just leave the table bare. Can you spare $1.99? That's the usual going price for a spray of white pompon mums. Now, two dollars' worth of pompons doesn't look like two cents in the middle of a table. But strew them from one end to the other, in miniature containers at each place setting, and they'll look like a whole month's pay.

Use demitasse cups (they don't have to match), inkwells, or even baby food jars or pill bottles for your containers. Or tuck your flowers into shiny polished apples—the juice will keep them fresh. Or forget the containers. Poke the mums into fancy-folded napkins or simply toss them on top of gaily printed napkins. Nothing looks more go-for-broke than flowers *out of* water.

Suppose you don't have even $1.99 to spare. Who wants an old-hat floral arrangement anyway? Whip up a "now" centerpiece with millions of candles in different sizes and shapes, or fancy bottles, or all your old bowling trophies, if you like. Remember, you're the girl who "always has flowers all over the house," and you can get away with anything.

9

The "One-Flower" Arrangement

WHO DID YOU WANT TO BE when you grew up? Florence Nightingale, the "lady with a lamp"? Lana Turner, the "sweater girl"? I wanted to be Mary Lasker, New York City's "flower lady," philanthropist, and wife of the late Albert D. Lasker. When her husband asked her what she wanted more than anything, she said, "Fresh flowers every day of my life"—and she got them. When I was younger, of course, fresh flowers meant to me a whole boxload from the florist's or armfuls from the garden. I don't know how many years I spent waiting wistfully for Mother's Day and Easter before I finally got the message—smart flower arrangers don't need *flowers*. I know it sounds crazy, but it's true; the older and wiser arrangers get, the fewer flowers they use.

Three's a crowd

Study the flower-arranging books in your library and you'll see what I mean. For every bountiful overstuffed Victorian bouquet, you'll find dozens of simple one-flower designs. The Japanese, of course, have been "flower arranging without flowers" for centuries. For one thing, they've had to—they don't have the big, sprawling gardens we have. But, more than that, they have too much reverence for all growing things to cram their material together into a bowl.

But one-flower arrangements don't have to be Japanesy. They don't have to be screamingly avant-garde, either. They can even be Victorian—what is a bud in a bud vase? At their best, they're as natural and naive as a water lily in a pond. Don't let the arty blue-ribbon arrangements in flower shows and textbooks scare you. Forget about rules and do your own thing. Remember that one single, perfect flower is an arrangement in itself, and almost anything else you come up with will be a plus. Think small. Once you get over your all-or-nothing complex, you'll be surprised at how much you can do with "nothing."

Guess how many glads

Please note that "one-flower" is in quotes in the chapter heading. That's because "one-flower arrangement" is a catchall phrase for any arrangement that has fewer flowers than you'd expect. When most people think of floral bouquets, they think in terms of dozens, right? To me, "one-flower" means anything short of one dozen, so don't haul me into court if you count four, six, or even eight tulips in my bowl.

But let's take the arrangement of glads at the beginning of this chapter. How many flowers do you think are in it? There are exactly three (at thirty-three cents per glad). In case you read the Introduction, which nobody ever does, here are your "three cheap glads," as promised, with which to dazzle your dinner guests. The trick is to cut them short and mass them instead of standing them in a vase like sticks. (For a step-by-step diagram and instructions, see pages 10–11.)

As you can see, three glads are really all you need, especially when all those buds open up. But if you want to gild the lily, tuck in some glossy green leaves or add a few tendrils of ivy. For extra dazzle, add purple cabbage leaves and a dangle of shiny black grapes to pink glads with a pink candle. If you have two silver candy dishes, you might even squeeze a pair of arrangements out of the budget (reverse the triangle in the second).

Everybody's doing it

You'll learn in Chapter 14 that the one-flower look is "in." But you won't catch the posh New York florists puttering over pink glads in silver compotes. They like the natural look—*two* day lilies in a basket of tomatoes or *three* zinnias in a burlap bag. In fact, all the Beautiful People like to keep their flowers simple. Hair-stylist Vidal Sassoon floats three perfect gerbera daisies in a glass of water (". . . a *bouquet* of gerberas is merely beautiful"). Gloria Vanderbilt Cooper always has a single anemone on her elegant desk. Fashion designer Geoffrey Beene uses nothing but understated, naturalistic "little nothings" by florist MacDonald Forbes.

Another popular New York florist, Robert Miglio—with a whole shop to raid—takes home only one or two of his pet lilies or ranunculi when *he* entertains. Jewelry designer Kenneth Jay Lane likes lilies, too—but just a sparse handful (he fills up the table with lots of toothpicks in interesting holders). Hostess-extraordinaire Dorothy Rodgers, wife of the famed composer, says, "To me, little bouquets just big enough to catch your eye as you pass a table or desk are most appealing. And these often take three or four blooms, not a dozen."*

So show me

You've found one-flower ideas all through this book. That's what it's all about—how to use green leaves, branches, weeds and grasses, fruits and vegetables, dried materials, art objects, and "found" objects so that you don't need a dozen flowers. But one-flower arrangements are harder to visualize than, say, a bowl

* *My Favorite Things* (Atheneum Publishers, New York, 1964), p. 79.

of apples or a clump of branches in an umbrella stand. And if you're like most people, one-flower arranging makes you nervous. Perhaps the best way to get you started on your one-flower career is not with a lot of vague chatter but with actual arrangements. (You'll find the complete low-down on the suggested containers in Chapter 13, but to make life simpler—a spill is a tall cylindrical container; a dish is any low, shallow bowl; a pillow is brick-shaped; and a compote is a footed bowl.)

The "basic black dress" arrangement

Before you do anything else, make yourself what I call a basic black. This is a practically permanent background of long-lasting greens, driftwood, dried materials, rocks, or whatever that you can accessorize over and over. Just plop in a flower or flowers as they come your way. You'll save hours and hours of arranging time. In between flowers, make do with succulents, "groceries," other fresh greens or dried things, maybe a small flowering houseplant. Or put the thing in storage so you don't get sick and tired of it. There are hundreds of basic blacks you can concoct, and they don't have to be ultramodern, either. True, most garden clubbers build their "permanent" arrangements around trusty old driftwood or manzanita, but here's an ultratraditional basic black that would probably fit into ninety percent of America's homes. You can move it from dining room table to buffet to mantel to front hall. What's more, you can use it all year round. Here, the "backbone" of fresh magnolia leaves and white pine (in a large

Oasis block on a low platter) is brightened for winter with snowy-white mums. In the spring and summer, substitute any feathery fresh foliage such as podocarpus or lycopodium for the pine, and replace the mums with garden flowers or fresh fruits. In the fall, use blazing marigolds or chrysanthemums and sprigs of bright autumn berries, perhaps with aucuba instead of magnolia.

At Christmastime, go right back to your pine boughs or any other favorite evergreen. Use pinecones in place of flowers and tuck holly berries and sliced pinecone "flowers" here and there. If you're really tired of looking at your basic black by then, go all out and spray the whole thing gold. Then start another!

Fifty, count 'em, fifty one-flower ideas

(1) In a seashell, float one pink rose or peony.

(2) In a brown bean pot, arrange three yellow marigolds with dock and dried magnolia leaves.

(3) In a melon-half, poke one well-budded day lily into greens from the florist, garden or refrigerator.

(4) In a brandy snifter, plant one flaming red poppy or anemone and snippets of huckleberry leaves.

(5) In a shrimp server, arrange one red geranium and geranium leaves; tuck sprigs of parsley where the ice should go.

(6) In a compote, stand one bare bough of hawthorn with three red tulips just over the rim.

(7) In a martini pitcher, stand two budded stems of iris surrounded by iris foliage.

(8) On a flat, round plate, make a tussy-mussy (that's an old-fashioned lace doily bouquet) with tulip and ivy leaves, feathery fern, and three pink tulips.

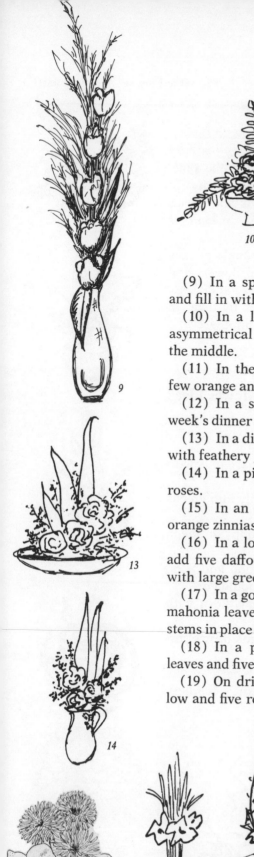

9

10

11

12

(9) In a spill, arrange five red tulips stepping-stone fashion and fill in with Scotch broom.

(10) In a low compote, arrange three leafy branches in an asymmetrical triangle and cluster three orange gerbera daisies in the middle.

(11) In the center of an inverted copper ring-mold, place a few orange and yellow zinnias in a water glass.

(12) In a spill, perch the last, lone red carnation from last week's dinner party in a soaring bare branch.

(13) In a dish, stand three graduated sansevieria leaves; soften with feathery juniper and add three roses.

(14) In a pitcher, rearrange the same sansevieria, juniper and roses.

(15) In an orange-painted pie plate, stand a squatty glass of orange zinnias and heap fresh lemons around it.

(16) In a low container, stand a bunch of tied daffodil leaves; add five daffodils around the outside, and cover the pinholder with large green plant leaves.

(17) In a goblet, combine three roses with pussy willow stems, mahonia leaves and croton leaves (use chicken wire to hold the stems in place invisibly).

(18) In a pewter pitcher, arrange three curving aspidistra leaves and five red tulips.

(19) On driftwood, arrange two aspidistra leaves, pussy willow and five red tulips.

13

14

15

16

17

18

19

20

21

22

23

24

(20) On a compote, make a rosette of hydrangea leaves; fasten the short-stemmed remains of a mixed bouquet with a rubber band and stand off-center on a pinholder.

(21) In a spill, place two branches of hemlock, one high and center, one low and to the right. Fill in the middle with three orange day lilies.

(22) In a glass set into a larger hollow-stemmed champagne glass, arrange short-cut lilacs in a pyramid; fill the stem with florets of lilacs, too.

(23) In a low dish, arrange one white peony on a bed of shiny black coal; garnish with feathery fern.

(24) In a glass brick, arrange one stem of iris and three "contorted" iris leaves (see Chapter 6).

(25) In three cruets, stand three anemones—red, purple, and pink.

(26) In a cup-holder on a mirror, arrange magnolia grandiflora leaves in a spiral with one white spider mum.

(27) In shiny Christmas ornaments (anchored with a dot of floral clay), tuck sprigs of pussy willow or gay dried flowers.

(28) In a root, arrange three mums, Scotch broom and ivy.

(29) In a dish, arrange one stem of iris and five iris leaves; cover the holder with rocks.

(30) In a glass brick, arrange six tight tulips in a triangle. Fill in with three open tulips and curled aspidistra leaves.

25

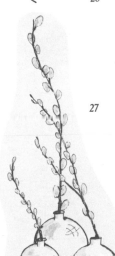

26

27

30

29

28

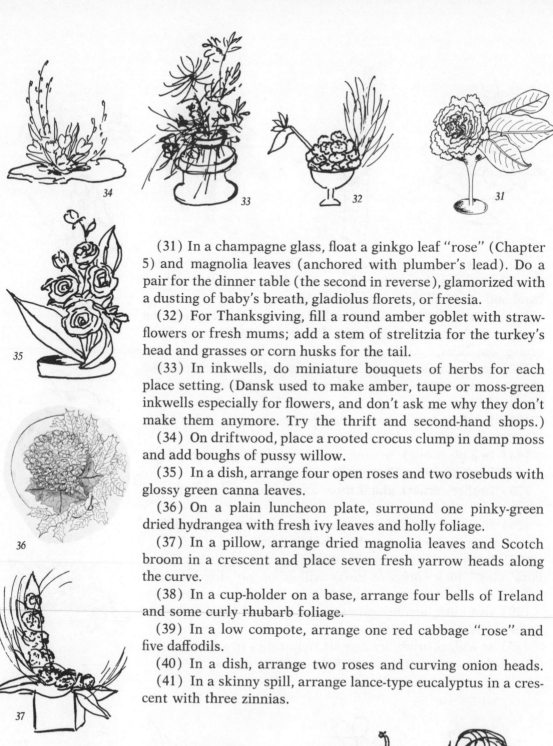

34

33

32

31

35

(31) In a champagne glass, float a ginkgo leaf "rose" (Chapter 5) and magnolia leaves (anchored with plumber's lead). Do a pair for the dinner table (the second in reverse), glamorized with a dusting of baby's breath, gladiolus florets, or freesia.

(32) For Thanksgiving, fill a round amber goblet with straw-flowers or fresh mums; add a stem of strelitzia for the turkey's head and grasses or corn husks for the tail.

(33) In inkwells, do miniature bouquets of herbs for each place setting. (Dansk used to make amber, taupe or moss-green inkwells especially for flowers, and don't ask me why they don't make them anymore. Try the thrift and second-hand shops.)

(34) On driftwood, place a rooted crocus clump in damp moss and add boughs of pussy willow.

(35) In a dish, arrange four open roses and two rosebuds with glossy green canna leaves.

(36) On a plain luncheon plate, surround one pinky-green dried hydrangea with fresh ivy leaves and holly foliage.

(37) In a pillow, arrange dried magnolia leaves and Scotch broom in a crescent and place seven fresh yarrow heads along the curve.

(38) In a cup-holder on a base, arrange four bells of Ireland and some curly rhubarb foliage.

(39) In a low compote, arrange one red cabbage "rose" and five daffodils.

(40) In a dish, arrange two roses and curving onion heads.

(41) In a skinny spill, arrange lance-type eucalyptus in a crescent with three zinnias.

36

37

38

39

40

41

42

43

44

(42) In five assorted glass containers, place five white petunias in different lengths and bloom size. (Or scatter them at each place setting for an instant table decoration. Never think petunias are strictly a bedding plant!)

(43) In a pewter cup, arrange one dahlia and five dahlia leaves.

(44) In a wineglass, arrange two roses and one rosebud with their foliage.

(45) On a compote, arrange six gladiolus florets with rosebuds for centers and green foliage.

(46) In a dish, arrange cattails, one monstera leaf and two calla lilies.

(47) In a palm spathe, arrange three tulips and tulip leaves.

(48) On a plate, arrange iris leaves, variegated hosta leaves and one echeveria rosette.

(49) In an Oriental compote on a base, stand five blades of yucca, needled pine, and two brilliant mums.

(50) In a seashell, set hosta leaves a-sail with a few geranium leaves.

50

49

48

41

10

How to Buy Flowers

EVEN POOR GIRLS who have to flower-arrange without flowers need a florist. In fact, they need two—one for the flush weeks of the year and one for the other lousy fifty. The trouble with most flower shoppers is that they don't shop. No matter what they need, they go to the same little florist across from the office or next to the dry-cleaner. It may not be the best shop in town, and it's probably not the cheapest, but it's there. That's no way to buy flowers when you're on your uppers.

Finding a bread-and-butter florist

Every town has one cheap-cheaper-cheapest florist. All you have to do is find him. The first place to look is the supermarkets. What you're looking for are buckets and buckets of mums and glads, usually sitting on the floor by the apples and onions. Any

133

old store sells daffodils in the spring and poinsettias at Christ-mastime, but you want a store that sells flowers all year long. Apparently, garden-oriented grocery chains differ from state to state. In suburban New York, I could always count on Shopwell. Here in Maryland, the best bet is Giant Food Stores. In California, I hear it's Safeway. (I've never met a flower-happy A&P yet. It may be where economy originates, but not eucalyptus.)

Good old Giant. Giant has eucalyptus—also anthurium, strelit-zia, Scotch broom, and other garden-club goodies. In addition to buckets of blossoms on the floor, there's a whole icebox filled with cut flowers and florist's greens. The beauty of *that* is that you can buy your flowers one by one instead of by the bunch. You can go flower shopping with a quarter! Best of all, you can pick your own flowers, and take all day to spend your quarter if you like. Nothing's as cheap as it used to be, but here's a typical late-winter price list:

Glads, 33¢ each
Anthurium, 99¢ each
Asters, 19¢ each
Bird-of-paradise, 99¢ each
Carnations, 43¢ each, $4.99 dozen
Iris, 39¢ each
Marigolds, 25¢ each
Redhot poker, 39¢ each
Roses, 79¢ each, $8.99 dozen
Sweetheart roses, 43¢ each, $4.99 dozen
Calendula, $1.99 bunch
Spider mums, 69¢ each
Football mums, 69¢ each
Snapdragons, 39¢ each
Peter John mums, 39¢ each
Ginger, 99¢ each
Tulips, 39¢ each
Statice, 15¢ stem
Giant daisies, 39¢ each
Stock, 39¢ each
Eucalyptus, 15¢ each
Asparagus fern, 10¢ stem
Baker's fern, 10¢ stem
Lemon leaf, 19¢ stem

Scotch broom, 29¢ stem
Pompon mums, $1.99 bunch
Daisies, $1.29 bunch

You can see why I love Giant. But if you can't find a super-market with a soul, look for a local fruit-and-vegetable stand. Most will have bedding flowers and potted plants in season, but some sell cut flowers the year round, most likely at cut prices. Your next best bet is a self-billed cut-rate flower store. If you haven't stumbled on one yet, don't bother looking in the yellow pages. Cut-rate stores aren't dignified by the term *Florist Shop*. Ask the nearest garden clubber. If there's a hole-in-the-wall in town that sells cheap glads or short-stem mums, you can bet she'll know about it.

And there's always the street-corner vendor. Unfortunately, America isn't one big open-air flower mart, like Europe. Our hus-bands don't come home with a loaf of bread under one arm and a bouquet under the other. But in our neck of suburban Baltimore, you'll find flowers for sale on every other corner. Even on winter weekends, red-cheeked boys and girls stand watch over buckets filled with bright-colored flowers to tempt passing motorists. I'm not sure the prices are rock-bottom, but they're not top-dollar either, and it's a merry way to flower-shop.

How to outsnoot a snooty florist

Bargain flowers from bargain shops aren't always your best buy. Sometimes it pays to go first class. If you're buying greens, they'll be fresher at a top-notch florist's and may not cost any more. If you need a particular flower for a special arrangement, a fancy shop will order it for you. If you're splurging to impress your husband's boss or your old college roommate, it's safer to splurge at a flossy florist. On the other hand, if you're making do with only three gerberas, why not treat yourself to the very best?

Would it embarrass you to ask for three gerberas in a lush-plush floral shop? Do snooty florists always make you wish you'd had your hair done first? Take a lesson from the pros. Flower arrangers never buy things by the dozen—they buy by the ones, threes, and sixes. What's more, they don't take the first flower that comes over the counter. Any garden clubber knows how to outsnoot the snootiest florist. "Sorry, that rose is too far open." "Oh, dear, don't you have any *fresh* chrysanthemums?" "No, no —I said orangey red anemones, not orangey pink."

You don't have to be obnoxious, but just don't apologize for letting them take your money. Another thing—don't forget that the flowers you see in the showcase are just the tip of the iceberg. Ask to peek in the refrigerated storerooms out back. Most garden clubbers insist on it. Aside from the sheer joy of seeing and smelling floor-to-ceiling flowers, it's fun to watch the shop's arrangers busily at work. Florist's shops are always busy, but some days are busier than others. Use your good sense and don't ask for special treatment on a frantic Saturday afternoon.

Fancy is as fancy does

As I mentioned in the chapter on greens, florists' prices vary astonishingly. Don't assume that if carnations are $1 at Florist A, they must be $1 everywhere. Florist B may have them for 75¢, and Florist C for $1.50. Don't be surprised if the fanciest, supposedly most expensive shop has the cheapest carnations. And don't be too sure that the most-expensive-in-fact shop has the freshest carnations.

As a case in point, recently *New York* magazine ordered $15 worth of cut flowers from twelve different Manhattan florists. Frankly, not one of the assortments looked like $15 to me, but the difference between them was fascinating. They ranged from "skimpy," "funereal," and "exhausted-looking" to "absolutely beautiful and very fresh." The worst-looking bunch came from a shop in Grand Central Station (beware of buying flowers on the fly!). The best-looking bunch, to my mind, came from the ever-elegant Plaza Hotel. The editors—and I—concluded that you'll generally get more for your money at a fancy, well-known shop than from a small neighborhood florist.

Would you like to know what $15 buys in New York City? At one shop: eight measly carnations, six puny roses, eight tired stock, and a smattering of leatherleaf fern—plus $2.50 delivery charge. But here's what the Plaza Hotel florist sent: four carnations, three irises, two roses, three gerberas, three tulips, three anemones, six daisies, pittosporum and leatherleaf foliage, plus a pack of Floralife—and no delivery charge. (Don't forget—that was yesteryear. Who knows what, besides Floralife, you'd get for $15 today.)

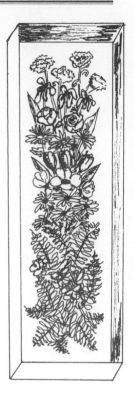

Don't let your fingers do the walking

The editors of *New York* ordered their flowers by phone, which I hope you wouldn't dream of doing. In the first place, you have to order a minimum amount. In the second place, you have to pay for delivery. Even in uncosmopolitan Maryland, one florist charges $2.50. Worst of all, you can't see what you're getting until it's too late. But suppose you're sending flowers to someone else. Don't, if you can help it; *take* them. At today's prices there's no such thing as sending a "little thank you" to your dinner hostess or a "little remembrance" to a sick friend. The average price for a small arrangement is $12.50, plus delivery and tax. If you insist, a shop will grudgingly make up something for $8.50. Even a dinky "dish garden" runs around $8.00. Why spend all that money for a gift that will probably look just like four others next to it on the hospital windowsill? Wouldn't your friend be just as happy with a gay do-it-yourself basket? If she's a real flower lover, she'd be even happier with one perfect bloom in a bud vase.

I never leave a thrift shop without every basket and bud vase they've got. At 10¢ and 25¢, what do I care if I never see them again? Cut-rate import shops such as Pier One are another good source for inexpensive baskets, bud holders, mugs, jars, and other containers. Why not drop off a handsome bread basket filled with fresh fruits by way of a bread-and-butter note? Why not deliver your own pottery dish-garden filled with thrifty green plants from the five-and-dime? Even if you don't have flowers from your own garden, you'll still save a bundle by buying and arranging your own. In the chapter head illustration, you'll see what you can get for $8.50 at the florist's (plus delivery) and what you can do yourself with $1.29 worth of daisies. (To make your own professional-looking bow, simply loop the ribbon several times and wind florist's wire tightly around the middle. Wire it to the basket handle or to a florist's pick to stick in potted plants.)

Be your own FTD

Sending flowers out of town is a little stickier. It would seem that FTD and Teleflorist have you over a barrel. The cheapest arrangement you can send is $10. That's $10 for three roses in a bud vase, or maybe eight carnations. On top of that you'll have to pay the sales tax, the cost of the intercity phone call, and a service-and-delivery charge. What's more, there's no guarantee that the arrangement you chose will arrive exactly as pictured. I'm not knocking FTD, *but*—I don't like their prices, I don't trust my friends to tell me what their flowers looked like, and I hate to send people containers that I wouldn't have in my house.

What to do? Eliminate the middleman. Call the florist yourself, in New York, California, Ohio, or wherever. How do you know whom to call? Unfortunately, long-distance Information will not thumb the yellow pages for you. You'll have to outsmart her. First, ask for the "name of town" florist shop—there's almost always one listed. Next, try The Flower Box or Flowers by Michael. Every town has a Flowers by . . . somebody, and while she's looking for Michael, she's bound to blurt out Martin or Olaf. That's all you need.

When you've got your man, make it crystal-clear that you're calling long distance (and try to call after five o'clock or on weekends). Tell him what you want, ask him what he's got, and settle on the best value for your dollar. Loose flowers or a flowering plant are probably best, but if you decide on an arrangement, request a plain old basket. Even if you don't reach the best florist in town, you'll know what you're getting and you'll get it for less, phone call and all. How do you pay for the flowers? Florists are nice people by trade. Over the years, I've had only one florist balk at billing a perfect stranger by mail (but he was happy to accept BankAmericard).

It's even cheaper to order flowers by mail. Do you have a faraway mother-in-law to whom you send flowers regularly? By all means, get the name of her favorite florist and write ahead for her Mother's Day, Easter, and birthday flowers. Be sure to enclose a hand-written card with your order. The florist will give you special attention, your mother-in-law will be astounded by your forethought, and you'll be dollars ahead.

Tiptoeing through the petunias

Chances are you won't buy annuals and potted plants at the same place you buy cut flowers. You need still another florist, or twelve. Luckily, in the spring, "florists" sprout on every corner. You can trot from garden center to five-and-dime, vegetable stand to hardware store, supermarket to farm, nursery to department store to find the cheapest petunias, healthiest marigolds, or biggest selection of impatiens. Plant booths at church, school, and garden-club bazaars are another good bet. Even better, if you live in the suburbs, are wholesale farms. You may ferret out the same wholesaler who supplies your favorite retailer, and save as much as half. Look in the classified section of your local papers, too, for people who have perennials to sell.

Remember that petunias are always cheaper by the flat. Pots are for rich girls. And don't be tempted to buy the tallest plants with the most flowers in bloom. Pick short, fat, stubby ones with no flowers if you want bigger plants later on.

When you're buying flowering plants like mums and azaleas, wait till after a holiday—look for half-off sales after Mother's Day, Easter, and Thanksgiving. And don't snoot the green houseplants in dime stores. You'll find lots of exotic species that just need a little time to grow.

Be your own florist

Expert flower arrangers never have enough greens, but they don't run to the florist for every sprig and twig. They grow their

own. Instead of buying expensive new plants, they start new ones from the old. It's called propagating. To most people, propagating is what rabbits do so well. The very term *plant propagation* scares the average girl to death. But it's one of the easiest poor-girl tricks I know.

Thanks to the plastic-bag makers, now every girl can have a "greenhouse." For 99¢ you can buy 75 gallon-size Glad Bags, with 75 twist-ems thrown in. Or you can use plastic bags from the dry-cleaner. The only other equipment you need is: a plastic tray, starter soil, Rootone, and a wire coat hanger.

Here's all you do: in June or thereabouts, take six-inch cuttings (without flowers) from your favorite shrub. Remove the bottom leaves, dip the tips in water and then Rootone (to prevent mildew), and plant them. A favorite rooting mixture is one-half peat moss and one-half vermiculite. Wet it well and give the cuttings an extra spray before covering. Two crisscrosses of bent wire, fastened with a twist-em where they meet, will keep the plastic tent upright. Close the bag tightly to keep moisture in, set it away from direct sunlight, and forget it. When the cuttings have rooted (about eight weeks), open the bag gradually each day for a week before potting or planting in the garden. Keep shaded for a week or so. Before you know it, the baby plants will be as big as their mother.

This is the softwood-cutting method, and it's practically foolproof for any broad-leaved evergreen in your garden (or, better still, a friend's)—azalea, holly, boxwood, rhododendron, euonymus, mahonia, laurel. You can also take softwood cuttings from perennials such as chrysanthemum, coleus, geranium, lantana, sedum, and summer phlox. Once you get the propagating bug, you can bone up on other methods in the library—hardwood cuttings, layering, and air-layering.

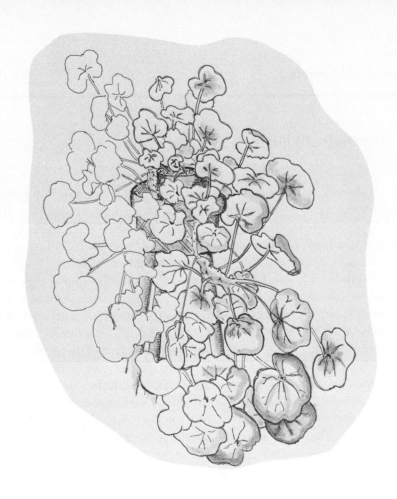

The penthouse propagator

City girls (and lazy girls) can play too—even if they don't have a backyard full of shrubs or house-room for a dozen plastic tents. Taking leaf cuttings from houseplants is the easiest trick of all. Simply put a healthy leaf with about two inches of stem in water. Use a narrow-necked Coke bottle or cut a slit in plastic stretched over a glass. Some quick-and-easy plants to root are African violet, gloxinia, peperomia, echeveria, sansevieria, kalanchoe, bryophyllum, and streptocarpus. If you don't know whether you own any of these jawbusters, start with a begonia. Anybody but anybody can root a begonia. A few years ago I carried an orphaned "beefsteak" begonia leaf around one whole hot afternoon before I got it home into water. Here is that leaf today. What's more, it now has children and grandchildren from California to Connecticut, because I give a leaf to every visiting fireman who admires it. Imagine if I talked to my plants! I don't, nor even feed them.

The Perfect Florist

For now, you can't afford to be a one-florist woman. You have to play the field if you want 99¢ flats of petunias, half-price tulip bulbs, and three-foot tomato plants for $1.99. But some palmy day you may want to settle down with one perfect florist, one "verray, parfit gentil" florist. Here's what to look for:

Look for a florist for all seasons, a florist who's all things to all flower lovers. Look for a florist with greenhouses—greenhouse after steamy greenhouse—that you can meander through blissfully, with the boss or on your own. Look for a florist who has both bouncing baby annuals and gorgeous grown-up perennials—both teeny pots of ivy and towering rubber trees—both 50¢ begonias and $50 hanging baskets. Look for a florist who grows his own flowers, and has for the past fifty years. Needless to say, look for a florist who has all this plus the best florist's shop in town—the kind that will sell you anything from one piece of Scotch broom to the whole works for a wedding and let you mosey around the cold-storage rooms out back till your ears drop off.

If you haven't found the perfect florist yet, keep looking. He exists. I know. If I never get to Heaven, at least I've been to Radebaugh's.

11

Make Your Flowers Last

===================

BEGGARS CAN'T BE losers. When poor girls get flowers, they have to keep them—and keep them and keep them. Obviously, the longer your flowers last, the fewer days you'll be flowerless. So, when the florist throws in a freebie pack of Floralife, use it. It's not just a silly frill; it's a modern, scientific preservative that really works. I can't tell you how it works, because Floralife and its cousins are close-mouthed about their secret formulae. I suspect that it mostly kills germs, because it's germs that mostly kill flowers. Nor would I bet on its adding "five to ten days more life for your cut flowers," but why cavil? I'd settle for even one extra day. You can also buy liquid preservatives that promise, more modestly, to "extend the life of cut flowers." One, called Prolong, is usually around at Christmastime because it also helps keep the needles on your Christmas tree. But who needs fancy commercial products? Wait till you hear all the old-wives' tricks that wise arrangers know.

145

Never at noonday

The first order of business is to get your flowers off to a healthy start. That means picking them in the cool of the morning or the cool of the evening, never during the heat of the day. It also means picking them before they're already on their last legs. Most flowers should be picked just as they open. Pick bulbous types when barely half open, and grab roses, poppies, and peonies while still in bud. A few flowers, such as iris and day lily, can be picked either in bud, half open, or just open. If you've ever had the notion that garden flowers snipped in the bud will be nipped in the bud (i.e., never open up), it's just not so. They bloom as merrily in a vase as in the garden.

As soon as your flowers are picked, pop them into the bucket of water you've lugged along. Tripping through the garden with a Victorian gathering-basket hooked over your arm makes a pretty picture but doesn't do a thing for your flowers. Serious arrangers have nifty custom-made carriers fitted out with an assortment of containers, but never mind—a cheap plastic pail is all you really need. If you want to keep your tall flowers, short flowers, and prize specimens safe and separated, just drop a few appropriate jars into the bucket.

"Butterflies" aren't free

You've probably heard that household scissors are a no-no for cutting flowers. In fact, you've probably been told that a sharp knife is a must-must. Well, razor-sharp knives are okay on a cutting board in the kitchen, but in the garden? Actually, nothing beats a good pair of clippers for indoors or outdoors. Look for the Japanese type called butterfly clippers. Garden clubbers love them.

Butterfly clippers aren't cheap ($5 and up) but they're efficient, and think what they'll do for your flower-arranging image. If you get the kind with natural raffia handles, paint them with bright red nail polish pronto so you won't keep losing them in the grass. One day when mine were lost, I switched to ordinary pruning clippers and have stuck with them ever since. Some experts frown on them, but I like them even better than "butterflies."

Suppose you're picking flowers at the florist's? Once again, early morning is best. The choice is wider and the flowers are fresher. Florists do their level best to keep flowers in tiptop shape, but obviously some flowers have to be older than others. Don't be shy. Ask for the flowers that came in just this morning, not yesterday or the day before. Ask for flowers in bud, please, not full-blown blossoms. And don't assume that florist's flowers have been properly pretreated and that all you have to do is plunk them into a vase. Experienced arrangers don't trust anybody. As soon as they get their flowers home, they condition them just like garden flowers.

What's "conditioning"?

Conditioning is simply garden-club talk for what you do to flowers to make them stay fresh longer. It's also called *hardening*. It includes things to do before you arrange them and things to do after. Actually, there are dozens of special rules for special flowers, but let's begin with general good hygiene.

As soon as you bring your flowers in from the garden or home from the florist, recut the stems on a slant—*under water*. The air bubbles you see will tell you why. The less air in the stem, the more room for water. Water cutting, or *mizu-giri*, is the ancient Japanese method of prolonging freshness for several days. Next, strip off any leaves you don't need, especially those which will be under water in your arrangement. Plunge the flowers almost to their chins in lukewarm water, as illustrated at the beginning of the chapter. Place them in a cool, dark place for several hours or, better still, overnight. This is what's known as the deep soak. If you don't plan to arrange your flowers for several days, you can put them in the refrigerator. Hopefully, you have an old castoff in the basement that you use for beer, the Thanksgiving turkey, and, now that you're a flower arranger, flowers.

Are you confused about hot and cold? If refrigeration is good for flowers, how come you soak (and arrange) them in warm water? Remember that, when it comes to water, flowers are just like people. They don't like an icy-cold shower or toe-scalding tub any more than you do. Room-temperature water is best. But refrigeration is something else again—it simply slows down nature's workings and so prolongs a flower's life.

Keep it clean

When it's time to arrange, remember that cleanliness is definitely next to godliness. Be sure your container is clean enough for a baby to drink from, and scrub up your pinholder even if it kills you. Germs are as bad for flowers as they are for people. Put water in the container *before* you arrange, fill it when you're through, and add more a few hours later if needed (it's called topping-on). Some flowers, like phlox, are incredible guzzlers and should be topped-on in an hour or two. Only a purist would change the water every day, but at least add some fresh water daily. For either job, a turkey baster is the handiest tool ever invented. You can slurp up old water or squirt in new without mussing up your arrangement or spotting your furniture. An occasional squirt with a flower mister helps (do it in the kitchen and *blow* off the drops afterward), and try to remember to move the arrangement to a cool place before you go to bed.

Treat 'em rough

Forget what you've learned about razor-sharp stem cuts, deep-soaking, and gentle lukewarm baths. Here come the exceptions that prove the rule. Believe it or not, it's better to break brittle stems of mums and snapdragons in your hand than to cut them. Thick, woody branches of flowering shrubs should be split and crushed (a meat tenderizer is good for this). In fact, lilacs thrive on sheer brutality. Break the stems when flowers are in bud, strip off all the leaves, then scrape, strip, or hammer *hard* about five inches up the stem.

Did you know that some flowers actually don't like water? Daffodils are happiest in a shallow two inches. Three to four inches of water is enough for irises, lilies of the valley, pansies, sweet peas, gerbera daisies, cattails, and horsetails (equisetum). Succulents, of course, need no water at all; just an occasional misting. I've also heard that the best way to condition violets is to mist them and wrap them in damp newspaper. Incidentally, tulips should always be wrapped in newspaper before setting them to soak—and rewrapped and resoaked every night, if you really love them.

Some like it hot

Then there are flowers that like their water hot. When you pick zinnias, daffodils, delphinium, and baby's breath, try running the stems under hot water first. Even more important to remember are the oddballs that like their feet *burned*. The "famous four" are peonies, poppies, dahlias, and hydrangeas; others include fuchsia, forget-me-nots, clematis, lilies of the valley, and gloriosa daisies. To condition them, either hold the stems in boiling water for several minutes or char them over a candle flame. Charring is

quicker—and easier on both you and your flower heads. If you want to live dangerously, set fire to a rolled-up newspaper and singe your stems in the hot ashes. Supposedly, giving flowers a "hotfoot" opens up their pores so they can drink faster. After a heat treatment, put flowers in cold water.

Speaking of drinking, flowers love a hot cup of "tobacco tea" when they're tired and droopy. To brew tobacco tea, crumple one cigarette's worth of tobacco into a pint of hot water and let it steep before adding your flowers. You can also add a pinch of tobacco to the arrangement water. Another old-fashioned shot-in-the-arm for tired flowers is the "steam bath." Here again, it's no fun standing over a hot stove. Instead, pour boiling water into a tall container and make a collar out of newspaper to protect the blossoms. Or stick funnels into Coke bottles for individual flowers. Even roses will usually revive with this shock treatment.

More old wives' tricks

I'm sure you've tried dosing your flowers with aspirin or sugar and wondered if it was worth the trouble. Chances are, it was. Aspirin, sugar, alum, even a dash of Clorox—all help to slow down nature and to keep flowers fresher. Rubbing dry sugar into dahlia stems also helps. But aspirin and sugar are kid stuff. Have you ever tried oil of peppermint, rock salt, Karo syrup, hydrochloric acid, baking soda, candle wax, egg whites, or alcohol, not to mention that ole devil gin?

I can't begin to list all the old-timey remedies I've picked up from newspaper articles, books, flower-arranging teachers, and garden clubbers, but here's a sampling of fascinating favorites. I won't swear that I've tested all of them, or that I use any of them faithfully. Frankly, I think they're more fun to read about than to do. But what can you lose? Even if one little flower lives one more day, you're ahead of the game.

CARNATIONS   Rub table salt or dry boric acid into ends of stems; place in boiling water for three minutes and then soak in cool water. Recut stem ends (between nodes) every day.

DAHLIAS   Spray daily with fine mist of ice water.

ZINNIAS   Soak in 2 tablespoons rock salt to 2 quarts water.

GLADIOLI   To hold for a week, buy them in bud and store in a covered box on a cold floor; then cut ends and soak in warm water.

MARIGOLDS   Stand in ¼ teaspoon oil of peppermint to 1 quart water for four minutes, then deep-soak as usual. Add 1 tablespoon granulated sugar to arrangement water to reduce odor.

DOGWOOD   Stand in 2 teaspoons gin to 1 quart boiling water for three minutes, then deep-soak in cold water.

SNAPDRAGONS   Stand in 3 tablespoons baking soda to 2 quarts water. Change arrangement water every other day.

LILIES, PEONIES, MUMS   After charring stem ends, turn upside down under a cold shower. Be careful to keep inside of flower dry. Remove stamens from lilies to keep from staining everything in sight.

ROSES   For garden roses, place stems in boiling water until water cools, then in 5 drops wood alcohol to 1 quart water. For florist's roses, soak in 2 teaspoons sugar plus 2 teaspoons salt—or a pinch of alum—to 1 quart water. Roll in newspapers and submerge completely to soak.

PETUNIAS   Pick long stems with both flowers and buds; condition overnight in 5-percent solution of sugar and tepid water.

POINSETTIAS   Stand in 10 percent solution of hydrochloric acid and water for five minutes, then deep-soak.

IRISES   Cut in bud and sear ten minutes in hot ashes, or let stand three minutes in boiling water; then deep-soak.

FREESIAS, FORGET-ME-NOTS   Stand in 1 teaspoon alcohol to 1 quart water for one to two hours.

WISTERIA   Cut after sunset and stand in 20 percent solution of alcohol and water for five minutes; then deep-soak.

POPPIES   Drip matching-color melted candle wax into bloom at base of petals after flower has opened.

TULIPS   Drop white of egg onto tips to keep them from opening. Add ½ ounce calcium nitrate to 1 quart arrangement water.

GERANIUMS   Spray the back with hair spray.

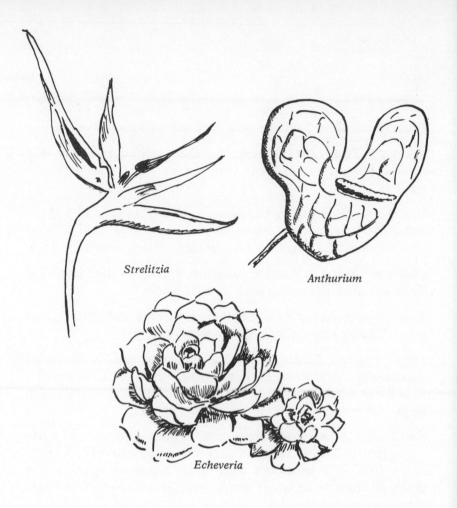

Strelitzia

Anthurium

Echeveria

Here today and here tomorrow

When you have to watch your pennies, it's only common sense to pick rough, tough, sturdy flowers that won't hate themselves in the morning. All the conditioning in the world won't make a tulip go as far as a tiger lily. From the florist, your very best bets are carnations, anthurium, calla and other lilies, gladioli, stephanotis, and bird-of-paradise (strelitzia). Among garden flowers, you can count on mums, zinnias, irises, day lilies, and marigolds. Many of these will even last for hours out of water if you condition them well first. Don't forget that you can stretch glads, snapdragons, and lilies for weeks if you pick them partially budded. Just snap off the faded parts and use them down to the last floret. And need I remind you of the greatest long-distance runners of all—the succulents, such as echeveria?

Part Three

How to Flower-Arrange Like a Garden Clubber

12
Tricks of the Trade

THERE'S ONLY ONE THING WORSE than not having flowers—that's having flowers and not knowing what the heck to do with them. Why do you think the florists sell all those rip-off, ready-made arrangements? Give the average girl a beautiful box of cut flowers and she falls apart. What is she going to put them in? How does she get the darned things to *stay put?* Why, oh why, doesn't her bouquet look like the ones in magazines and at flower shows?

The answer, of course, is that the girl doesn't know her "mechanics." Mechanics is garden-club talk for how you put an arrangement together and what you put it together with. Mechanics is what you *don't* see (perish forbid) in a blue-ribbon arrangement.

Do you know all about florist's clay, florist's wire, and florist's water picks—not to mention turkey basters, pipe cleaners, potholders, and tuna fish cans? Do you know how to make a short stem long and a straight stem curvy? Can you doctor a broken stem, revive a droopy flower, or mend a moth-eaten leaf? Read

155

on. The reason flower arranging drives you to tears is *not* because you're clumsy, stupid, or unartistic—it's just because you don't have the right tools.

Those pointy things

In case you haven't heard, the be-all and end-all of flower holders is not your mother's thirty-year-old glass "frog." What you want is a pinholder, which may also be called a needle or needle-point holder. At any rate, it's that heavy green metal gadget with all the spikes you see in flower shops, hardware stores, and the five-and-dimes. Don't get plastic, and be sure the pins are very close together. Good pinholders aren't cheap (about $2 for a leaded, rustproof "Dazey" in the favorite three-inch size), but don't be tempted to make do with just one. Get yourself a slew of them. If you have to search for hours for your one-and-only buried in the basement under last month's dried arrangement, you'll be licked before you start.

Pinholders are the surest, safest, sturdiest flower holders going. Dedicated arrangers keep a whole wardrobe on hand, practically one for every container. Which is lucky for you, because when containers end up in the thrift shop, they frequently come complete with pinholder. I've picked up half a dozen that way for nickels and dimes.

How come people give away costly pinholders with their unwanted containers? Because they can't get them out. Don't think you can just plop your holder in a container and be done with it. You have to *anchor* it, if you don't want your arrangement to lean, lurch, or fall flat on its face after all your hard work. Here's

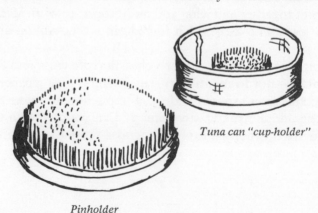

Tuna can "cup-holder"

Pinholder

where the florist's clay and potholder come in. First, be sure that everything is bone-dry—clay, pinholder, container, and your hands. Pull off a piece of clay and roll it in your hands till it looks like a snake. Wind it around the bottom of the pinholder, grab a good, thick potholder and *lean hard*, with a slightly circular motion. This will seal it so that no water gets in and also secure it to the container. You should be able to turn your container upside down and shake it without budging the holder.

Actually, getting a pinholder out of the container isn't all that hard, but many garden clubbers sidestep the problem by anchoring the holder to a blah-type bowl. The blah-type bowl can then be whisked in and out of fancier bowls or containers. Instead of a bowl, the out-and-running favorite for this purpose is a lowly tuna fish can. It's a perfect liner for smaller containers, and not-so-small ones if your family uses the giant thirteen-ounce size. Paint it black and it becomes a "cup-holder" for noncontainer arrangements (i.e., things drifting on top of driftwood), with a bit of foliage for camouflage. Metal caps from aerosol cans make good cup-holders, too.

Even with a Gilbraltar-type pinholder your troubles aren't over. Suppose your flowers have skinny, hair's-breadth stems that simply refuse to be impaled? Instead of climbing the wall or going out for new glasses, chop off a piece from another fatter stem and poke the puny one in. You're bound to have throw-away ends lying around the sink. But be sure that the bottom stem is right side up, the way it grows. Stems won't drink if they're upside down; it's against their photosynthesis. Another solution is to bind groups of skinny-stemmed flowers together with florist's tape or a rubber band, or add clay to the holder. If you're wrestling with a thick, woody stem, crush it first with a hammer, or slice it across with your clippers.

One last word on pinholders: keep them clean. Aside from a soap-and-water bath, dig out all the debris with an icepick or metal skewer. If the "pins" become bent, straighten them with a pair of pliers or an old-fashioned clock key. Some florists sell a special Japanese gadget called a *ken-zon* that does both jobs. Incidentally, ordinary round or oval pinholders are the best. The fancy add-on and take-apart kinds sound like a better idea than they actually are—they tend to be tippy or to come unglued.

The foamy green stuff

Beginners are crazy about the water-holding chunks of poly-foam called Oasis, Quickie, and other names. So am I. Oasis is quick, easy, and fun to work with—at least the first time around. For many arrangements it's every bit as good as a pinholder. For some it's even better, because you can poke in your flowers every which way. In basket arrangements it's tops; just wrap it in foil and go to work.

Don't forget to soak Oasis first, of course—thoroughly. It doesn't take that long, even though florists charge you more for theirs because it's presoaked. If you cut your Oasis to fit the container, chances are it won't bobble around; but just to be sure, secure it with crisscrosses of waterproof tape.

The trouble with Oasis is that after it's done duty three or four times it looks like a hunk of moldy Swiss cheese. You can no longer place your flowers where you will; where you'll stick your flowers, chum, is where there are no holes. Worse than that, Oasis crumbles when it dries out. When you've paid $1 or so a block, on the theory that you'll have it the rest of your life, who needs a pile of pea-green sawdust? But if you're still hooked on Oasis, here's a little secret that hardly anybody knows: once it's wet, you have to *keep* it wet. Don't let it sit around in a half-dead arrangement that's waiting to be thrown out. Give it another good soak, and then pop it into a plastic bag with a tight seal. (Keep your florist's clay in a plastic bag, too.)

Chicken wire, sand, potatoes, and such

Garden clubbers have been using chicken wire for years—the same old-fashioned stuff you find in every hardware store. Different arrangers swear by different sizes, but the two-inch size works fine (technically it's turkey wire). Now there's a fancy green plastic-coated version called floral mesh. Whichever, it can't hold a candle to pinholders or Oasis, if you're a ruddy perfectionist.

Chicken wire holds, but only sort of. It's probably most useful in tall, columnar containers. Crush a wad for the top and fill the bottom with crumpled wet newspaper to help keep stems in place. Pull a few inches up over the top so you can slant your stems. For weight, put a rock in the bottom. Chicken wire is also good for clear glass containers; secure it just at the top. Some arrangers say that small pieces of evergreen boughs stuffed into a container are every bit as good as chicken wire. Or how about pretty rocks? Another good trick for clear containers is crisscrosses of Scotch tape that are practically invisible in a finished arrangement.

You can also use wet sand to weight your tall container. In fact, wet sand is handy in lots of ways. I use any kind I have around, but I suppose the sterilized playbox sand they sell in hardware and toy stores is kinder on flowers; it's also more accessible to apartment dwellers. For instant patio arrangements, fill clay pots with wet sand, stick in bright-colored candles, and surround with gay flowers. Not only pretty but practical—and no chance of fire. Dry sand, of course, is fine for dried arrangements of the casual type. If you're plotting something more elegant, you'll do better with dry Oasis or styrofoam (with sand at the bottom for weight and strips of tape to keep it in place).

Garden clubbers have all kinds of crazy gimmicks for particular flower-arranging problems. Suppose you're doing a footed compote of flowers and want to add some grapes. What you need is a potato—just an ordinary potato. Push the potato into your pinholder, wire the grapes firmly together with crisscrosses of fine wire, and dangle them from the Idaho with round toothpicks. Or suppose you have a bowl of fresh fruits and want to add some flowers. What you need are little orchid tubes or water picks from the florist (very cheap—usually no more than 3¢ apiece). Water picks are better, because you can anchor the pointy stick beneath the glass vial to your pinholder. You can improvise your own water picks with plastic pill bottles bound to tongue depressors with pipe cleaners.

If a favorite bowl is too deep for your flowers, anchor an upside-down tuna fish can to the bottom and fasten your holder on top with clay. If you have a heavy hunk of manzanita or driftwood, use extra wads of clay to wedge it in place. You can also buy a special manzanita holder at many dime stores for 69¢.

You might think that the bowlful of carefree daisies at the beginning of the chapter simply arranged themselves. Not so. The mechanic here is a Scandinavian-style "hand bouquet." Make a circle with your thumb and forefinger and drop in a handful of daisies, one by one, at varying angles and depths. Wrap the stems with floral tape. Continue adding rings of daisies, taping each group as you go along. The crisscrossed stems, cut to fit the con-

tour of your bowl, become an extra plus in your design. (You might also wonder why I'm forever drawing daisies. It's because they're my favorite flower. Field daisies, florist's daisies, garden daisies, supermarket daisies—I love them all.)

Meanwhile, back to the "frog"

See how simple it is when you know how? No? It all sounds like too much work for you? Forget I even mentioned mechanics —you don't need them anymore. The "arranged" look is out! The "natural" look is in! Read all about it in Chapter 14! Now you don't have to make flowers stay put—just let them all hang out. Now you don't have to follow stiff, stuffy rules—just arrange flowers the way they grow. In fact, guess what brilliant invention Bonniers has come up with? Our stupid, useless old friend, the "frog" (at $7.50 a throw).

Another Bonniers brainstorm is the Arranger. It looks like a mesh beanbag filled with crystal-clear marbles. At $3.25, I can't see hiding it in an opaque container, but it's fine for glass ones. I like it best out of water, as an instant "vase" for a few dried roses. Another version of the same is the Liberated Frog sold by Taylor & NG, 651 Howard Street, San Francisco, California 94105. These are loose glass marbles sold by the pound ($2.50 for a half pound, $4.75 for four pounds) in a round plastic container (or use your own). The company must be "liberated," too —they actually suggest using them to arrange dried weeds, branches, and grasses as well as fresh flowers. Marbles would also be more elegant than dirt or pebbles for forcing spring bulbs.

Well, amen and hallelujah to "natural" flower arranging. That's the only kind I like (i.e., know how to do). But I for one am hanging on to my pinholders. See this natural-looking little basket of cornflowers? It's so simple. It's so airy. No wonder it was a best-selling flower gift at Parrish-Woodworth in New York. But don't tell *me* it can be done without "mechanics." (P.S.: Guess what decorated the tables at President Ford's very first State Dinner? Baskets of blue cornflowers, delphinium and yellow mums. The china was the Johnson china rimmed with wild-flowers.)

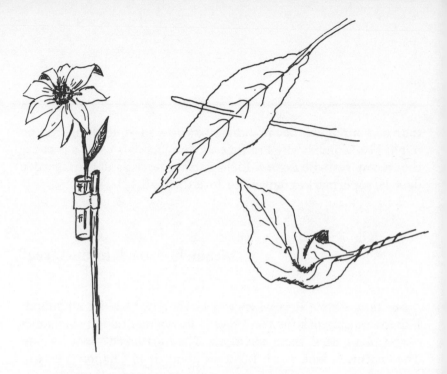

What to do till the doctor comes

The trouble with most beginners is that they're too lily-livered. They're scared to death to tamper with nature. If they have a sick flower on their hands, so be it. If they have a broken stem, out goes the whole flower. Poor girls can't afford to waste a single bloom, so here are some first-aid tricks from the experts.

In the first place, flowers aren't the fragile creatures you think they are. They won't scream if you touch them. Do you want a zinnia to turn its head a different way? Just take it in your hand and squeeze. Do you want a zinnia to stay fresher longer? Poke it in the joints of the stem with a darning needle. Daffodil fanciers spend hours manhandling their prize blooms for a show (they call it *grooming*)—stuffing cotton between the petals, ironing out each petal between their fingers till it's smooth as satin. And how do you revive a wilting rose? Plunge it into boiling water (the stem, that is).

Speaking of stems, of course they won't break if you bend them—if you know how. The Japanese do it all the time. I've watched a dainty arranger no bigger than a doll outmuscle a branch as big as she was. *Gentle but firm* is the watchword. And keep your two hands together when bending. Most flower stems will yield to patient, persistent pressure, but if you want to be sure they stay bent, you can cheat. Wind florist's wire or pipe cleaners around them. Would you like to change the curve of a leaf? Form a hairpin out of very fine wire and pull it through the veins in the middle of the leaf and down around the stem— now you can bend it any way you like. You'll find dozens of other tricks to do with leaves in Chapter 6.

But what about broken stems? You know and I know that it's always the biggest marigold or the fairest rose in the bunch that snaps its stem. So what you do is put a splint on it. Use a tooth-pick, florist's stick, or pipe cleaner and wrap with florist's tape. If the stem is too far gone to save, amputate—and slip the short stem into another long, hollow stem. Or use a pill bottle taped to a stick. This is also a good trick for the short-stemmed flowers that florists sometimes sell at bargain prices. Good hollow stems to use are lily, day lily, gladiolus, and celosia. Incidentally, never be afraid to cut a long stem short. Florists adore long stems, but arrangers think they're silly.

Flower arranger's first-aid kit

Aside from all the gadgets, tools, and gimmicks already men-tioned, every arranger should also have these things on hand— wire cutters, hand stapler, dowels, rubber bands, icepick, flower mister, raffia or carpet thread, charcoal (to keep water sweet), plumber's lead (to secure heavy branches in a tall container— twist a strip around the branch and hang it over the rim), mani-cure scissors (to trim flowers and leaves), cork floats (to float flowers on top of water), and moss (to hide your mechanics). The last two are sold in florist's shops and garden centers. If you grow your own flowers and have my bony knees, don't forget knee pads. Portable kneeling cushions are too much trouble, but most knee pads sold for gardeners are either too clunky or too expensive. Borrow your son's basketball pads (and scribble flow-ers on them with magic marker so he won't want them back).

The big thing to remember about mechanics is that *anything* goes just so long as it works—chewing gum, hairpins, linoleum paste, kitty litter, you name it. Who knows how many ingenious tricks of the trade have been kept from the world by their cagey inventors—or have yet to be invented. By you?

And did your mother ever tell you?

● Hide the telltale white end of a cut branch by rubbing it with cigarette ash.
● Change the color of a flower overnight by putting food coloring in the water (especially Queen Anne's lace). It will travel up the stems.
● Styrofoam is easier to cut with a wet knife.
● Shine up dull leaves with liquid shoe polish (natural, if you like, but brown is more interesting).
● Spray-paint dried material any wild color you like.
● If you don't have artists' acrylic spray to preserve a dried arrangement, hair spray will do.
● When you're measuring flowers for an arrangement, turn them upside down—it's much easier.
● If you want to mix dried and fresh flowers, use *two* containers.
● Use a turkey baster to slurp up the water in an intricate arrangement before carting it to a show or to a friend in the hospital (also good for emptying the water in your Christmas tree stand before you drag it out the door). For some reason, old-style metal basters have more cachet with garden clubbers than plastic ones.
● Instead of a big, loose bunch of tall grasses, dried yarrow, etc., bunch and tie them into small clumps—somehow they look better that way.
● Staple or wire decorative leaves (especially ginkgo) into flowery rosettes. Dip them in glycerin to keep them supple while you're working.
● Use a forked branch wedged into a tall container to keep tall stems or branches in place.
● Don't try to fold chicken wire—crush it.
● Bleach your materials, Japanese-style, by soaking in Clorox and water, then hanging in the sun (directions in Chapter 6).

- Dip fall leaves into melted paraffin and iron them between sheets of newspaper.
- Curl Scotch broom by wiring it into circles and soaking it for several hours.
- Use a funnel to arrange flowers in a narrow-necked vase.
- Open a tightly closed rose by breathing on it warmly and gently.
- Turn back the outer petals of a rose or tulip to make it more interesting (it's called *reflexing*).
- Spray finished arrangements with a flower mister, especially all-greens and frosty green-and-whites. Add a pearl or a glass chip here and there for drops of "dew."
- Check the refuse piles of glass works, iron foundries, steel mills, and rubber factories for arranging accessories.
- Spray "clinkers" of coal before using in arrangements.
- If you dig your own moss, bug-proof it first. (Moss can be purchased at florist's, garden centers and some dime stores.)
- Peel wisteria vines and other branches while they're still fresh.
- For easy skeletonizing, soak leaves in two tablespoons of Clorox to one quart of water for at least one hour. Rinse and wipe away remaining fleshy part with soft cloth. Press between paper towels for twenty-four hours.
- Curl skeletonized leaves by rolling around a pencil and holding over steam.
- HIDE YOUR MECHANICS! Use anything you like—moss, foliage, pebbles, rocks, fungi, shells, aquarium crystals, or pink and purple jelly beans—but never let anyone *see* all your clever little tricks of the trade.

13

But Never a Vase

To THINK HOW I used to scrounge for vases whenever anyone brought flowers to the house. To think that I even asked for vases one long-ago Christmas. Someone should have told me the first rule of flower arranging. To wit, you don't put flowers in vases, stupid; you put them in "containers."

That's the best news a poor girl could get, because you don't have to ask Santa for containers; you don't have to go out and buy them; you've already got them. What's more, containers take all the work out of arranging. Garden clubbers worship containers. To them, the container is half the arrangement. They're so busy ogling each other's bean pots and hollowed-out driftwood that they don't even notice the flowers inside. So throw out your vases, get yourself a kooky container—and you'll be halfway home.

Smaller than a bread box

Everybody knows the difference between a vase and a "vahse," but what's the difference between a vase and a container? A vase is what you get for a wedding present or buy at the five-and-ten. A vase, whether it costs under $10 or over, was designed to hold flowers and has no other use whatsoever. A container was designed to hold anything *but* flowers—coffee, tea, or milk; pickles, pencils, vitamin pills; baked beans, bath salts, umbrellas, goldfish —you name it. A container is anything and everything you've got that holds water, plus a few things that don't.

Look around you. You've got hundreds of flower holders you didn't know you had. To start with the most obvious, there are sugar bowls, cream pitchers, tea pots, coffee mugs, demitasse cups, and gravy boats. But they're not the half of it. You can use candy dishes, cake stands, jello molds, salad bowls, chafing dishes, soufflé pans, or vegetable dishes. You can use tea caddies, cigarette boxes, cruets, ice buckets, water pitchers, mixing bowls, cookie canisters, candlesticks, or apothecary jars. Anything goes, from your precious Tiffany baby cup to a humble aluminum watering can.

Strictly B.Y.O.B.

In the glassware department alone you have enough containers to last a lifetime—goblets, wineglasses, martini pitcher, liqueur glasses, tumblers, footed old-fashioned glasses, beer steins, sherbet dishes, shrimp servers, brandy snifters, champagne glasses, decanters. Never, never, throw out an old bottle or jar. A potpourri of assorted glass containers is one of the trendiest looks in arranging these days.

In fact, anything made of glass is "in." You'll read about Alvar Aalto's classic vase in Chapter 14. But you don't have to go the $80 route. Good-looking glass containers crop up every day in the stores. One clever new container is simply a see-through glass box with a removable plastic insert full of holes to hold as many or as few flowers as you like. It currently sells for about ten dollars, but it *used* to sell for sixteen, so keep your eyes out for a budget version. Even mail-order king Miles Kimball sells "exquisite, hand-blown Pilgrim glass vases to show off prized blooms" ($4.95 for either the four-inch or six-inch size). Actually, some of the most elegant containers today look just like chemist's flasks and beakers. The Glass American Company took note of that fact and sells a trio of tiny Flower Chemistry flacons for $6.95. Are they kidding? Why not ferret out a laboratory-supply house and buy the real thing cheaper?

Why spend even a nickel? You can do all the chichi see-through arrangements you want with old wine, whiskey, or cordial bottles, decanters, salad dressing bottles, spice jars, perfume bottles, airplane miniatures, medicine bottles, pill vials, baby food jars, or salt and pepper shakers. Last spring I practically furnished our living room with an assortment of flowers and branches in glass thingamajigs strewn on a French marble table. Because it was taking the place of an eight-foot white sofa that was out being reupholstered, I did it in all-white—flowering dogwood, spirea, white iris, peonies, lilies of the valley, and petunias. The stand-in arrangement did the job so well I was almost sorry when the sofa came back.

The garden-club Basic Four

To be honest, garden clubbers do use a few containers that might be called vases, and you'll probably want to, too. You can't improvise every day of the week. You need a few old faithfuls that you can grab with your eyes closed, like a trusty old dress in the closet. The trick is to know "bad" containers from "good" (most of the vases sold in shops should be thrown at the people who designed them).

Here are the four basic shapes that most experts agree every arranger should have: (1) the "dish"; (2) the "spill"; (3) the "pillow"; and (4) the "compote." (You'll notice that the "bowl" is conspicuously absent. *I* put flowers in bowls, *you* put flowers in bowls, but for some reason the experts don't.) With these four classics on hand, you can hold up your head in any flower-arranging circle. And you can reproduce almost any arrangement in the flower-arranging books.

Simple as these containers are, they're not always easy to find. The best places to look are Japanese shops, import outlets like Pier One, and better garden-supply stores. Department stores and fancy gift shops are the worst places to look. Try your local florist only as a last resort. He'll probably have the container you want, buried under eighty-nine others you don't want, but

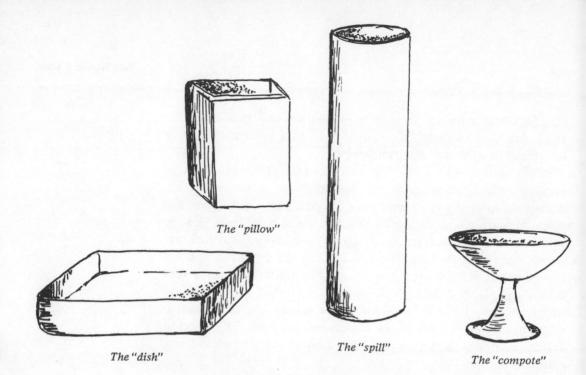

The "pillow"

The "dish"

The "spill"

The "compote"

at a high price. By all means try the thrift shops. Containers stream into junkshops at an alarming rate. Apparently, hundreds of flower arrangers die with no one to follow in their muddy footsteps. Another tip-top source for basic containers, as well as handsome and tasteful one-of-a-kinds, are local potters and other craftsmen. Better still, make your own basic four.

Pie plates, beer cans, and your old 78s

With a little know-how and a good can opener, you can turn the homeliest object into a garden-club container. For a dish container, a favorite trick of the experts is to spray-paint an old pie plate or rectangular cake tin. (Black on the outside and green on the inside is very garden clubby.) For a cylinder-type spill, use a tall coffee can—or two cans glued together for an even taller container. Other handy-dandies are forty-six-ounce juice cans, beer cans, and tall square saltine cans. Use a floor-wax can with the top removed for a pillow. You can paint your cans and tins, "antique" them, or cover them with contact paper. Sprinkle sawdust between paint coats for an interesting rough finish. You can also staple or glue on corrugated paper, bamboo or straw mats, and pieces of real bark. Or how about winding rope, yarn, or raffia around the can?

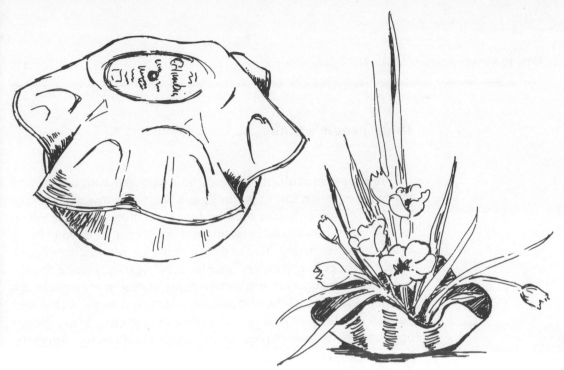

It only takes a minute to concoct a classic footed compote. Just upend a candlestick or goblet and set a bowl or plate on top. Add as many tiers as you like, secured with florist's clay. For pedestals, you can also use pieces of plumber's pipe, newel posts, or the furniture legs sold in do-it-yourself stores. And don't overlook your lazy Susan. For the contemporary look, use a plain white cereal bowl plus a plain white dish slightly off-center. The "flower" is a dried mullein rosette teamed with dried Scotch broom and leaves.

Once again, fruits and vegetables are perfect instant containers. Scoop out pumpkins, squash, eggplant, apples, oranges, or melons and add any household jar to hold water, or simply poke your stems into the juicy pulp. Save your berry, peach, and mushroom baskets, too. They're great *au naturel*, but with a coat of silver paint they could pass for the shiny, plaited tin baskets that are all the rage now.

Other good-looking do-it-yourselfs can be carved out of feather-rock, soft sandstone, or soapstone. Garden clubbers even make their own out of sheets of plumber's lead. And have you ever melted an old phonograph record for a container? Try it—it's kind of wild. Place the record on an inverted ovenproof bowl and heat at 250–300 degrees for ten minutes. It will fall into natural ripples, or you can bend it to suit. Cover the hole with florist's clay. (At 350 degrees, your old Artie Shaw will char and bubble into a hunk of "coal" to use as an accessory.)

Other people's junk

Junkshops are full of unloved, undiscovered containers, and it's twice as much fun to go junking when you know what you're looking for. What you're looking for is anything with a crack in it—old cups, bowls, pitchers, and pots of no use to anyone but a dried-flower arranger. You're also looking for interesting crocks, butter tubs, coffee grinders, mortars and pestles, candle molds, lamp bases, bird cages, umbrella stands, cookie jars, jugs, mugs, antique scales, coach lamps, powder horns, spittoons. A chamber pot is a real find; so is almost anything in copper or brass. Heavy hotel silver is sometimes surprisingly cheap—bun warmers, finger bowls, covered vegetable dishes, or dessert compotes. Even if you don't know what something is—especially if you don't know what something is—grab it. Who cares if it's the innards of an old ice-cream maker or a prehistoric sick-room vaporizer, as long as it makes a good container? Incidentally, antique sewing machines make dandy planters.

Junkyards are even better than junkshops if you're a dedicated arranger. I've seen everything from old stove tops to gas-tank caps turned into flower holders. Look for castoff builders' supplies, such as cement blocks. Chunks of slate can be used for bases.

Are bases necessary?

I'm sure you've noticed that half of the arrangements in shows and books sit on bases. The idea is that a base enhances, dignifies, or "completes" an arrangement. To my unenlightened eye, it merely ruins it. A base says, "Look, everybody—it's an Arrangement!" just as a light over a painting says, "Look, everybody—it's Art!" The only time I'd use a base is under an arty, abstract still life of fruit that I'd just spent an hour composing. Hopefully, a base would keep the whole family from digging right in because they thought my grocery bag had split open.

In any event, bases are a moot point in today's unarranged-look arrangements. But in case you're so inclined, the most revered bases are simple Japanese teakwood stands and handsome burls of polished wood. Garden clubbers would starve for a week for a really rare or custom-made base, but you'll find inexpensive ones everywhere. If you're not sure you're ready for bases, experiment with things you have around the house—bamboo and straw place mats, tiles, hotplates, trays, mirrors, or slabs of marble or slate.

Of course you can chop, stain, and polish your own burl. But for an easier homemade base, get a thick plywood board from the lumberyard. Paint, stain, or varnish it, or cover it with wood-grained contact paper. You can also tack fabric to a slab of styrofoam. Strips of bamboo lashed together make a Japanese-looking "raft." But the best makeshift base of all is an old breadboard. Simply stain it with black or brown liquid shoe polish and glue on spools, buttons, or pieces of dowel for legs.

Look, Ma, no water

The fun with containers really begins when you have dried flowers and grasses to play with. When you don't have to worry about water, the whole world is your container. First of all, there are baskets, beautiful baskets, in hundreds of different sizes and shapes. Collect baskets whenever and wherever you find them—you can never have too many. In the thrift-shop basket pictured at the beginning of this chapter, dried hydrangeas are simply tossed, not arranged, without even a water-filled liner. They're *Hydrangea paniculata* that in mid-August ranges from white to pink to pale chartreuse and dries beautifully just sitting there. But don't stop there. How about a straw hat or a bird's nest? I even used doggie donuts once, in a gag replica of the Baroness's "table landscape" described in Chapter 14. Then, of course, there's driftwood. With a little florist's clay and a pinholder, you can plant all the flowers you want in, on, and around driftwood. The same goes for shells, rocks, roots, tree stumps, fungi, and other found objects dear to garden clubbers.

But let's say you don't have any fungi lying around the house. In fact, let's say you're just a plain, ordinary flower lover who thinks fungus is horrendous. How about some fresh new ideas

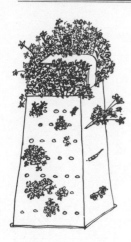

for old fogies? Okay, I'll start you off. Have you got a kitchen grater? Try studding a shiny, silvery grater with tiny hot orange, pink, and red starflowers. While we're in the kitchen, how about flowers growing out of your toaster, a colander, napkin holder, or even your everyday coffee pot? You won't be using them on party night anyway. A hanging French lettuce basket can hold anything from gaudy golden strawflowers to shiny red onions.

On to the next most florally neglected room in the house—the bathroom. What crazy no-water container can we come up with there? The toothbrush holder, of course. Ours happens to be a hand-painted Italian ceramic standing model, but I almost wish it were the usual motel-type chrome fixture on the wall. I can see it dressed for a party, with flowers tucked in the toothbrush holes and another bouquet where the water glass goes. Have you ever thought of a drawer as a container? Pull out the top vanity drawer just far enough to hold a lineup of gay potted flowers, fake or fresh—much more pow than a fortune in florist's flowers in a vase.

Now that you've got the idea, take a look around your living room. You might tuck a spray of flowers behind a painting on the wall, between the bellows by the fireplace, or into a bookcase or magazine stand. Why not have flowers sprouting from the "innards" of a baby grand or from a silver baby shoe? Heap a hurricane chimney with colorful fresh fruits or a kindling basket with pinecones. In fact, why not skip the container altogether? One of the most chic arrangements I've seen—the ultimate in no-water container arranging—was a sheaf of blue-green starflowers tied with a green velvet bow and simply tossed on a gleaming table.

Don't forget to use no-water containers to hold fresh flowers, too. To waterproof a basket, drop in a glass, bowl, or foil-wrapped cake of Oasis. Hide a tuna fish can cup-holder in a natural crevice of driftwood, or bury it *behind* your driftwood, root, shell or sculpture.

Nag, nag, nag

The most "in" containers today are baskets, burlap bags, clay pots, and glass beakers (see Chapter 14). But if you're shopping

for conventional containers, like the basic four mentioned earlier
in this chapter, don't make the usual beginner's goof. Steer clear
of busy patterns and strong colors—they're for people who don't
know any better or for absolutely tip-top arranging experts. Most
garden clubbers stick to muted, earthy shades of green, brown,
and gray. Black containers are very Japanese, but did you know
that white is the most difficult color to work with, and too risky
for amateurs? That was news to me, since white has always been
my first choice. Pigheadedly, it still is.

Above all, use the right size container for your flowers. That's
the whoppingest mistake that beginners make. Their containers
are always too big for their arrangements, or their arrangements
too small for their containers, whichever. Think tall and high and
out. Never have your bouquet the same size as your bowl. I
promised I wouldn't tell you how to arrange, but I must pass on
this one little formula. Your arrangement should be one and a
half times the height of a tall container or one and a half times the
length of a low container. (The size of an arrangement is mea-
sured from the rim of the container.) Believe me, it's not a silly,
arbitrary rule—it works. Try it and see if your next arrangement
doesn't look just like a garden clubber's.

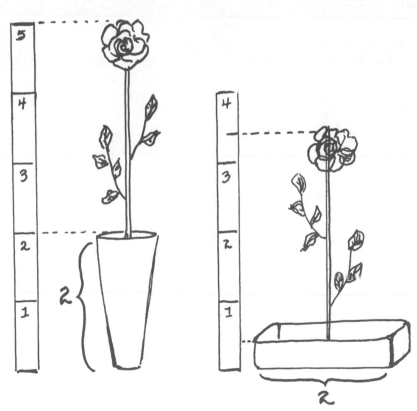

14
What's "In" and
What's "Out"

─────────────────────────

Do YOU KNOW the best way to look richer than you are? Jump the gun. Rush the season. Be the firstest with the newest. That goes for fashions in flowers as well as fashions in clothes. (Yes, fads in flowers come and go, too.) Never mind studying diagrams in books that were written when Grandma Moses was a kid. Never mind copying your neighbor's and your mother's dowdy old centerpieces. Start arranging like the Beautiful People. Remember, it's the rich who start new fashions in clothes, flowers, hair styles, vacation spots, and everything else. What the rich are doing with flowers today is what the rest of the world will be doing tomorrow. In fact, it takes so long for new ideas to filter down from New York penthouses to Peoria split-levels that you'll probably still be ahead of your neighbors five years from now, or even ten.

What "They" say about flowers

I'm sure you've heard of *Women's Wear Daily*, but you may not know about its glamorous weekly offshoot called *W*. You should, if you want to know what everybody who is anybody is wearing, eating, saying, doing—and putting in their vases. Not long ago, W* reported on the 1970s "revolution" in flower arranging, and I pass on the joyful tidings. Quoth W, "The art of arranging flowers has become much less formal and much more imaginative. If you have to make a choice between field flowers and a frontal arrangement, pick the field flowers. The natural look is in and ostentation is out." Hooray and hallelujah and what have I been telling you all along?

Just for fun and handy reference, here is, specifically, what's in and what's out:

IN:

Queen Anne's lace
Cow's parsley
Swamp candles
Grasses
Sunflowers
Black-eyed Susans
Loose, airy arrangements
Terra-cotta pots
One marvelous basket
Simple glass containers like a wide-based beaker
Alvar Aalto's classic vase
Crocks, especially old ones

OUT:

Orchids, except as plants
Gladioli
Carnations, except at Christmas
Poinsettias
Chrysanthemums, except for snowdrift
One-sided or frontal arrangements
Steuben glass
Lots of baskets
Cut-glass vases

*W, September 7, 1973.

Tall, urn-shaped vases with bases
Ceramic animal-shaped containers

Beautiful People bouquets

To find out where flower arranging is really at, *W* went to some
of the fanciest flower designers in New York City—Renaldo Maia,
Jean-Jacques Bloos, Bert Braff of George Cothran Flowers, John
Cianciolo of Parrish-Woodworth. Here's what the Beautiful Florists are putting on the Beautiful People's tables. "Big clay baskets
stuffed with dahlias in every color. Cornflowers and daisies for a
meadow look. A dozen bud vases in different heights that can be
grouped into different forms and shapes on a table—fill each with
a single iris. French wire baskets filled with real lemons with
English ivy and daisies coming up through the center. A bushel
basket filled with masses of spirea. Clay berry boxes filled with
cherry tomatoes and spiked with orange lilies." (Anything sound
familiar? Isn't it nice to know that all your tacky, poor-girl desperation tactics are the ultimate in chic?)

How about some "in" ideas in floral gifts? "Shallow clay sau-
cers planted with miniature ferns and croci [sic]. A small blue-
and-white English ironstone pitcher filled with grape hyacinths.
Real berry boxes planted with real strawberry plants just beginning to bloom. Real berry boxes planted with lilies of the
valley. Moss-covered cylindrical tin liners spiked with sprays of
tiny orchids or black-eyed Susans."

W's list of DO's and DON'T's

- DO use chicken wire instead of Oasis to hold flowers; it lets
the flower find its own balance.
- DON'T make your living room a showroom; have one well-
thought-out arrangement, not three or four.
- DO use dahlias, roses, peonies, and tulips for one-flower
bouquets.

• DON'T put pennies, aspirin, or sugar in your bouquets. It looks dumb.

• DO, if you have to, have a tall centerpiece; think of it as a see-through blouse . . . place a few tall flowers in the arrangement to establish height, then place some flowers deep, some out.

• DON'T be afraid to use a rustic container with weeds such as Queen Anne's lace, or just tulips in assorted colors, in a very formal room.

• DO use bouquets of one color in a modern interior, such as one great mass of marigolds, or all red tulips.

• DON'T put a huge arrangement—the kind that begins with a capital A—in a room with low ceilings. You'll have the feeling it's going to attack.

• DO remember that flowers are soft-looking; give them a container that lets them move.

• DO remember four things when you're arranging: space, color, texture . . . and surprise.

P.S.: Do it anyway

Now that you've heard what's in and what's out, just do as you please, please (at least you *know* better, right?). For one thing, "classic" vases by the great Finnish architect Alvar Aalto go for around eighty dollars. For another, there's nothing "dumb" about putting sugar in your bouquets, remember? If you still want to put carnations in your wedding-present cut glass, go ahead. And so what if too many bouquets spoil the decor? Maybe you like to see flowers all over the house and think it looks prettier that way. One suggestion, though: it's newer to cluster three or even six bouquets together than to sprinkle them round a room. Try it with dried arrangements, too. It's also newer to stick to one color, as *W* says—just as outdoors a solid planting of shocking-pink petunias is more chic than an old-fashioned English garden.

If you do mix your colors, break every rule about mono-chromatic, complementary, and analogous colors on the good old Munsell color wheel. Try what English arranger Sheila McQueen calls her "clashing" arrangements in wild oranges, reds, and purples.

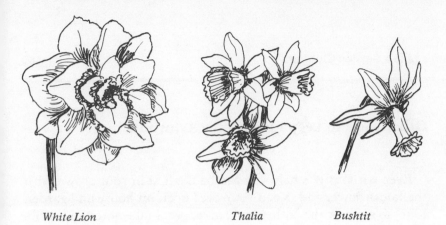

White Lion   Thalia   Bushtit

Are you tempted to play it both ways—the "in" way for company and "your" way for the family? Don't be a phony. If you keep your eyes and your mind open, you'll soon find your own style—a "new you" halfway between your old, trite arrangements and the newest look for the Beautiful People. Above all, remember the last word of *W*'s last DO—surprise!

The garden-club look

Chances are, you'll be entertaining more garden clubbers than Gloria Vanderbilt Coopers, so you should know some of their quirks and foibles. You already know that bare branches, driftwood, "all-greens," fungi, weeds, and dried things are "in." You know about their pet containers and the "proper" containers. You know they adore buds and baby green berries. It occurs to me that garden clubbers like everything *small*.

They're wild about dwarf evergreen trees, miniature iris, stunted lemon trees—in fact, the whole bonsai bit. They like little flowers better than big ones. They like single flowers better than double ones. For instance, huge formal-decorative dahlias are considered gauche, but dainty "collarette"-type dahlias are charming. Big, bulbous peonies are good-for-nothing in arrangements, but single types, like "Krinkled White" (it looks like a fake crepe-paper flower but smells nicer), are exquisite. Have you ever seen the double white daffodil, "White Lion"? It's incredible. It looks more like an overblown white peony than a daffodil. It sends amateur flower-showgoers into swoons, but, sure enough, daffodil fanciers turn up their noses. They'll take dainty "Thalia" (my very favorite, too) or funny little "Bushtit."

Other ways to keep up with the Astorbilts

Even without *W*'s help you can be the first in your crowd with the latest flower fad. Keep your eyes open on house-and-garden tours to see how the "other half" arranges. I take notes and scribble sketches all over the program. Check the room settings in department stores for bright ideas. Bloomingdale's and Macy's in New York are always crackling with clever notions, but big stores everywhere have talented, imaginative decorators and display people. (If you're a New Yorker, never miss a table-setting show at Tiffany's.) Go to flower shows, even though sometimes they're a little old-hat. (Garden clubbers have to go by the almighty Handbook, and you can't expect the Federation to rewrite *that* every year.) You may spot something new and different, and you'll surely pick up ideas on unusual containers and unfamiliar flowers.

Copy the pretty pictures

Most of all, steal from magazines—the dollar-and-up variety. Don't waste your time on the just-us-folks home magazines, and pay no attention to the ads in any magazine. I don't know who does the flowers for furniture companies, but I suspect it's FTD. (Pay no attention to Hollywood, either—I think they're still using Jean Harlow's flowers from *Hell's Angels*. Besides, someone told me that all movie flowers are fake.) Pore over the pictures in *Town and Country, House Beautiful, House and Garden, Vogue*, and such. You'll find fresh new ideas on page after glossy page. Take them; they're yours for the copying, in the dentist's office or library. The point is that once you know all about "mechanics," you don't need stuffy flower-arranging books with diagrams. What you need are some sassy, trailblazing ideas.

Be on the lookout for trends—they show up fast in decorating magazines. For instance, five years ago it was sacrilege to use a clear glass vase. You weren't supposed to let your nasty stems show. Today all you see in fancy room settings are see-through containers with stems in full view. Remember when feather flowers were all the rage? Neither do I, but those darlings of the thirties are coming back again. Are you still stuffing every flower you get into the most impressive "vase" you own? Now, if you'll notice, it's much smarter to scatter them into individual containers, as florist Stephen Barany does at the beginning of this chapter. (If you don't have expensive lead crystal, anchor your tippy glass vials with a dab of florist's clay.)

Notice all the unarranged arrangements around these days. High-priced decorator Michael Greer counsels his clients never to arrange their flowers, but simply to toss them. Notice all the houseplant arrangements, bare branches, and weeds (really an old eighteenth-century fad). Even at Christmastime, the back-to-nature movement is taking over. Instead of glitter, tinsel, and sequins, it's all fruits, berries, nuts, cones, tree bark, roots, herbs, and seashells.

You and the Baroness

By leafing through just a few magazines, you'll soon see which way the wind is blowing. You'll also get to peek inside the Beautiful People's houses, mansions, townhouses, penthouses, and chateaux. In case you missed one particular issue of *Vogue*, let me tell you about the flowers at Mouton, the French country home of the legendary Baron and Baroness Philippe de Rothschild (she came out in Baltimore, though). Actually, the Baroness doesn't use flowers on the table like ordinary people—she uses "table landscapes." She dots the entire table with weeds, grasses, green plants, and fresh flowers gathered from her gardens, greenhouses, and the surrounding countryside (gathered, I might add, by faithful Marie). On the following page is just one-third of a table with a "haunting, mysterious woodland fantasy" by the Baroness, but you get the idea. Now, you may not have all the go-with's the Baroness has (two huge household books full of swatches and photographs, with 170 patterns of china alone), but couldn't you come up with a table landscape, too? For the dining table or a cocktail table or even the mantel? (The illustration on page 48 is part of *my* haunting, mysterious seashore fantasy on a skinny mirror-backed mantel I never know what to do with.)

Stealing Sassoon's stuff

I've been borrowing groovy ideas from Vidal Sassoon for
years.* He's a hair stylist, of course, not a flower stylist, but he
thinks flower arranging is "groovy." I've already let you in on his
tricks with gerberas and apples and pebbles (Chapter 8), but here
are some more zanies. Instead of a humdrum centerpiece, line
up shimmering lab bottles in a diamond pattern and fill them
with yellow mini-carnations. Instead of the usual container, hide
a hunk of Oasis in a cluster of sparkly rocks and plant flowers in

* *House Beautiful*, November 1971.

it. Vidal's sparkly rocks were rock crystal, amethyst fluorite, and celestite sulphur (from Bloomingdale's, but also at gem and mineral shops); and his flowers were ethereal moth orchids, but you could make do with much humbler stones and common daisies. In fact, try florist Robert Miglio's nifty rock-candy trick. He piles it around a container of Oasis, and the reflection of the flowers by candlelight is spectacular.

This is my favorite Sassoon-steal: add shiny Christmas balls to the water in a clear glass container. In a tall crystal jar, Vidal used red balls, with a fortune in white hybrid *Speciosum rubrum* lilies —very Christmasy. I use silver balls in a fish bowl with five forty-nine-cent white spider mums—even in the summer. (If you start with red balls, they'll be silver anyway by the time they finish peeling, Vidal.) Incidentally, the editors point out that rubrum lilies will last two weeks or more in the vase, and after that you can stretch out the remaining fresh flowers in bud vases.

Extra, extra, read all about it

Believe it or not, flower arranging makes the newspapers and newsmagazines, too. Once you get the arranging bug, you'll find meaty tidbits of information everywhere. You'll read in *News-*

week that weeds are the very latest thing, as if you didn't know. But did you know that Lee Radziwill, Ali MacGraw, and producer Dino de Laurentiis are weed-people, too? Did you know that both the Nelson Rockefellers and the Ronald Reagans are proud owners of Alice Bingham "weed sculptures" in Lucite? And, in case you don't think the ancient art of flower drying is "now," one Atlanta expert was recently asked to dry a funeral wreath of mums and roses arranged in the shape of a guitar.

Read your newspapers and you'll learn that First Lady Betty Ford favors "innovative table settings" in the State Dining Room. She's also big on American arts and crafts and often borrows artifacts from museums around the country to use as the focus of her centerpieces. At a recent dinner party for the President of Colombia and his wife, she chose flower sculptures in porcelain from the Burgues studio in New Jersey. Designer Paul Lieborowski created "natural environments" for each piece out of fresh greens and other materials.

At a state dinner for the President of West Germany and his wife, Mrs. Ford used fruits and vegetables because "they love to eat." The table centerpieces were done by Robert Webb of New York, famous for arrangements of vegetables, fruits *and very few flowers*. Incidentally, rubber trees that have languished in the White House greenhouse for years have now been trotted out for "greenery without cost." See? You don't have to be poor to be thrifty. See? You don't have to be freaky to love weeds and vegetables. See what good company you're in when you start flower arranging *without* flowers?

Author's Postscript

NEEDLESS TO SAY, mum (*Chrysanthemum rubellum*) is the word. Whatever you do, don't tell your friends about the divine little flower-arranging book you've found. Hide it in your underwear drawer where only professional jewel thieves will find it. Especially don't tell your mother-in-law. But if she suddenly starts putting Christmas balls in fishbowls and anemones in the john, you'll know the jig is up. She's read the book, too, and you'll just have to start flower arranging *with* flowers.

Good Books
to Read and Own

Emily Brown, *Bouquets That Last*. Hearthside Press, Inc., 1970.

Katherine M. Cutler, *From Petals to Pinecones*. Lothrop, Lee & Shepard Co., New York, 1969.

Emma Hodkinson Cyphers, *New Book of Foliage Arrangements* and *Fruit and Vegetable Arrangements*. Hearthside Press, Inc.

Marjorie J. Dietz, *The Concise Encyclopedia of Favorite Flowering Shrubs*. Doubleday & Company, New York, 1963.

Jean Hersey, *Wild Flowers to Know and Grow*. D. Van Nostrand Company, Inc., Princeton, New Jersey, 1964.

Eloise McDonald, *The World Book of House Plants*. Popular Library, New York, 1963.

Phyllis Pautz, *Decorating With Plant Crafts and Natural Materials*. Doubleday & Company, New York, 1971.

Patricia Easterbrook Roberts, *Simplified Flower Arrangements*. Viking Press, 1960.

F. F. Rockwell and Esther C. Grayson, *The Rockwells' NEW Complete Book of Floral Arrangements*. Doubleday & Company, New York, 1960.

Stanley Schuler, *How to Grow Almost Everything*. M. Evans and Company, Inc., New York, 1965.

Norman Sparnon, *The Poetry of Leaves*. John Weatherhill, Inc., Tokyo and New York, 1970.

Index